YOU, YOUR HEIRS

AND YOUR ESTATE-

—

AN APPROACH TO ESTATE PLANNING

OTHER BOOKS BY GEORGE BYRON GORDON

USING TAX MONEY FOR THE FAMILY: A PRACTITIONER'S GUIDE (Prentice-Hall, Inc., 1962)

PROFIT-SHARING IN BUSINESS AND ESTATE PLANNING (Farnsworth Publishing Company, Inc., 1970)

With James C. Wriggins

UNDERSTANDING FEDERAL INCOME, ESTATE AND GIFT TAXES (Institute for Business Planning, 1952, 2nd Edition 1955)

REPAIRS VS. CAPITAL EXPENDITURES (Ronald Press Company, 1958)

With others

ESTATE TAX TECHNIQUES (Matthew Bender & Company, 1973)

YOU, YOUR HEIRS

AND YOUR ESTATE

AN APPROACH TO ESTATE PLANNING

by GEORGE BYRON GORDON

© 1962, 1973, 1977 by Farnsworth Publishing Co., Inc.
All rights reserved.
Revised 1977.
International Standard Book Number: 0-910580-13-8.
Library of Congress Catalog Card Number: 62-21861.
Manufactured in the United States of America.
No part of this book may be reproduced without
written permission from the publisher.

FARNSWORTH PUBLISHING COMPANY, INC.
78 Randall Avenue
Rockville Centre, N.Y. 11570

FOREWORD

Everyone who earns money possesses a potential estate.

The components are diverse. Everyone, just about, has earnings or salary, Social Security benefits for oneself at retirement or disability and for one's surviving spouse and minor children. Many of us also enjoy employment fringe benefits ranging from hospital and medical expense plans to complex security and thrift plans, and from the use of cars or other facilities to stock options. Hopefully these "assets" will be *in addition* to adequate personally provided life insurance, bank accounts, investments in stocks, bonds, mutual funds or real estate—and for some among us, equity holdings in our own businesses.

A man's earnings—the product of his effort—are partly income and partly capital, just as the returns produced by a machine are in part earnings and in part a return of cost or invested capital that must be set in reserve to offset depreciation of equipment. In the case of the machine, this accumulated depreciation plus the amount that can be realized upon the used machine itself is calculated to be enough to pay the cost of new and efficient equipment. In the case of a man, the reserve accumulation should be enough so that interest earnings upon it yield annually the difference between what he will need to maintain a reasonable standard of living and what he will be able to earn in full or semi-retirement. The accumulated reserve, then, is the estate to which a man may look for support when he is no longer able or willing to support himself entirely by his own efforts. It must be sufficiently great to throw off income, either in the form of income alone or in the form of a carefully calculated combination of income and capital to provide that support.

While everyone who earns money possesses a potential estate, the potential becomes an estate in the full sense only when something conscious is done to establish the separate, economic identity of the capital. What is done is not very important. It may be the opening of a bank account, the payment of a life insurance premium, or the placing of a dollar bill under a loose brick in the fireplace.

But whatever the components may be, the usual common denominator is that the estate available for support at retirement is less adequate than that becoming available at death. The gap arises because personal earnings tend to rise more rapidly than earnings upon invested capital; because many people rely too heavily upon employment benefits—i.e., pension plans, group insurance arrangements—and too lightly upon accumulations created only by their own self discipline.

Knowing what can be done, being consciously aware of it, and then doing something about it are the twin keys. Conscious awareness of what can be done, plus a move to establish it in fact, creates an estate. Certainly there are differences in size, in the efforts made to increase substance or wealth, and in the success attendant upon those efforts; but the estate exists as a separate economic entity from the time of the first act to convert the potential into the actual.

This business of giving substance to an estate, of gathering together an endowment independent of continued activity, is each one's own obligation to himself and his family. No one can do it for you, only with you by counselling and guiding and needling.

CONTENTS

PART III — TRANSFERS OF PROPERTY

PART IV — LIFE INSURANCE

PART V — FAMILY PLANNING

PART I
PRINCIPLES OF PLANNING

CHAPTER I

THE SIX UNDERLYING PRINCIPLES

An estate is not static. It is a living thing that develops and changes as the needs and status of its owner grow and change. At the beginning, the usual estate comprises the various kinds of property acquired mainly with an eye to probable increases in value and enrichment of the owner. Gradually, the emphasis shifts from getting more wealth to using the existing property as a source of income for living purposes. As the needs of the owner change from a main objective of further accumulation and more wealth to that of income for current living, the nature of the investments in the estate must also change. Speculative assets must be largely replaced by investments assuring continuity of income and security of principal. Planning is required.

Part of the planning is concerned with the disposition of property before and after the death of the estate owner; but the process as a whole goes far beyond that. Estate planning involves the creation of a standard and pattern of living for everyone, beginning with the estate builder himself, who will be dependent upon the estate. For that reason, estate planning begins most logically with careful consideration of the people whom it is to benefit.

The usual practice is to relax and merely to let things happen. Then circumstances, isolated impulsive actions, responses to momentary pressures govern the form and nature of the estate. Ultimately, a tiny fraction of the time and energy that went into the accumulation of property is devoted to planning distribution to heirs. Under those conditions, the basis of disposition is usually the property available, not the needs of the heirs themselves. The most frequent result is the imposition of hardship, economic disability, and frustration upon the heirs. Often the actual benefits that could be derived from the estate are canceled out by the lack of a thoughtfully developed plan.

The alternate method suggested in these pages demands more thought, time and energy—but its results are much more satisfactory in terms of both human and economic values.

Estate planning, like a circle, is endless. There is no beginning, as such, and no end. One cannot start, as in most other tasks, at a fixed point and follow logical, orderly steps to a pre-determined end. One cannot merely assemble data as to the end in view and then rearrange the facts and materials so that the desired result must be attained.

Then how do we begin? What must we do and when must we do it? The answers are to be found in the application of these six underlying principles, which we develop further in this book:

Principle 1: The needs of those who are to benefit from the estate and the desires of the planner for their comfort and welfare are the most important considerations.

Principle 2: The people who will share in any estate must be properly conditioned or trained if they are to obtain the greatest possible benefit.

Principle 3: The true measure of the value of assets is not net worth but income-producing power.

Principle 4: The assets of the estate should be distributed between fixed-dollar obligations that will pay in any event and equity or ownership assets whose yield is dependent upon earnings. The distribution should be in such proportions as to assure continuous income whatever business conditions may be.

Principle 5: Self-liquidating investments—assuring scientific distribution of both principal and interest over any given pre-selected period—should be used to put a stop-loss on capital invasions when:

a. Accumulated wealth is not quite sufficient to produce adequate future income in the form of interest or dividends; or

b. Time, taxes, or other uncontrollable factors make the accumulation of sufficient income-producing capital improbable.

Principle 6: Unnecessary tax liability must be avoided by the untiring and skillful use of all available legitimate means.

Principles 1 and 2 relate to people. After all, an estate is supposed to give people some measure of security, dignity, and pleasure. To provide these things even in small degree, we must know the needs of those who are to be benefited by the estate and the desires of the person who is planning for them. To get the utmost out of the estate, the beneficiaries must know precisely what they face and what materials they will have to work with. They must have some measure of skill in the use of those materials. If the estate resources are limited, the people who will share in it should know that and know the exact degree to which they will have to earn in order to live. If the estate is substantial, perhaps those who will share in it should be taught the finer points of property management, investment, and the conservation of capital. The nature and size of the estate itself, the physical condition and ability of the individuals to be trained, and the economic and social circumstances of the family determine the nature and extent of the training.

Principles 3, 4, and 5 relate to property. It is self-evident that the true measurement of assets is not net worth, but income-producing power: a truth that is emphasized when the estate owner reaches retirement or dies. Then the spendable income yielded by the estate must replace, insofar as possible, the earned income upon which the family previously relied. Similarly, no one would dispute the continuous need for income and the desirability of having a reasonably stable amount available from year to year for living purposes. Since the purchasing power of money varies so that it is lower in good times and higher in bad, stability of income depends upon a balanced distribution of estate assets between fixed-dollar obligations and equity or ownership assets.

The fixed-dollar obligations yield income of set dollar value without regard to earnings. The equity or ownership assets produce yields entirely dependent upon earnings. Thus, establishing and maintaining proper balance between fixed-dollar and equity assets tends to provide a reasonable, continuous level of income through periods of inflation and deflation, boom and depression. Reason: The equity assets produce more dollars in periods of higher earnings—and so partly compensate for the reduced purchasing power of the dollar—while the fixed-dollar assets produce a predictable flow of dollars whose purchasing power tends to increase in periods of deflation or depression when earnings fall off. Equities, of course, present a greater element of risk than fixed-dollar obligations, such as bonds and debentures; but their tendency to increase income yields in the estate portfolio—and so to offset to a degree the loss of personal earning power—may well compensate for that.

Clearly it is wise to use self-liquidating investments or annuities that serve to distribute principal and interest over a preselected time instead of relying upon haphazard invasions of capital in order to bolster inadequate income. All too often, people attempt to struggle along on too little income, relying upon the fact that every once in a while a capital asset can be sold and the proceeds used for day-to-day living. The hope is always that these capital invasions can be held to a minimum and that the bulk of the estate can be preserved for others. But that hope is apt to be false. Each invasion leaves less capital to produce income and further reduces the available income. Each invasion must be made at the time when funds are most urgently required—usually when the market is not at its best. Each capital withdrawal is apt to signify the sale of one of the choicest assets, since they are the most readily salable and bring the highest price.

It makes more sense to put a stop-loss order on capital invasion by consciously taking whatever percentage of the capital is required and investing it in an annuity that will produce enough return to bring the income of the estate up to the necessary level. That provides an outside limit on the amount of capital consumed and a guarantee of spendable dollars that will keep flowing so long as there is need for them.

But there is still another application of the principle of self-liquidating investments. Annuity or self-liquidating investments may be bought during the estate accumulation period. They may be annuities acquired in small fully-paid chunks or on an annual premium plan that calls for a regular deposit each year. They may be life insurance policies intended to be paid to beneficiaries as income over a term of years or for life—that is, to be self-liquidating investments maturing at death. Either way, they provide a means for accumulating capital and interest in a tax shelter and applying the entire accumulation, without depletion by income taxes, to the production of income at maturity of the contract. Used in that way, self-liquidating investments substitute a modern system of accumulation and scientific distribution of principal and interest over the period of need for the more old-fashioned method of accumulating capital and holding it intact to yield income.

Principle 6 relating to tax saving and the avoidance of unnecessary tax liabilities simply applies sound business concepts. Any skillfully and efficiently performed plan of operation takes into account the cost basis of the procedure selected. Proper application of this principle requires constant awareness of possible tax liability, but subordinates the saving of taxes to the accomplishment of the planner's primary purposes. Tax-saving considerations weave in and out of every phase of estate planning; but should rarely be the sole basis for any procedure. Too often, the choice is between a method offering the greatest possible tax economy in return for dangerous inflexibility and other methods, costing somewhat more in taxes, but offering greater freedom to meet changing business and economic conditions. Since the basic object of estate planning is to satisfy the needs of people and since we must do our planning in a rapidly changing world, it should be obvious that tax saving is just one consideration and that greatly increased flexibility and adaptability are worth a moderate increase in tax cost.

The six underlying principles of planning just discussed are applicable to estates of any size. All lie at the roots of any estate plan, whether the amount of property is modest or fabulous. In fact, they establish a pattern of thought for all planners, regardless of the stage of development of their estates or the extent of their resources.

One further word of warning. Estate planning is a large field. It requires the coordinated efforts, knowledge and intelligence of the attorney, the investment expert, the life underwriter, the accountant, and the trust officer. Each of these can make a very definite, specific contribution. All of them can and should work together harmoniously in the best interests of the client. There is no reason for discord or suspicion as, in the end, an efficient and satisfactory job of planning will usually be rewarding to them all.

CHAPTER II

PEOPLE

People are the most important considerations in estate planning.

Webster defines an estate as: "A person's property in lands and tenements or, in the aggregate, loosely, fortune; possessions.' He defines an endowment as: "That which is bestowed or settled on a person or an institution." Perhaps, for our purposes, the two definitions should be combined into: An estate is an endowment for living purposes.

It follows that planning a particular estate is tailoring it to provide some measure of security and comfort for specific individuals who will share in it. That goes far beyond the mechanistic concept of "this is what I have and this is what must be kept, so damn the consequences", and deals with the very stuff of life itself. Thus all planning should start with consideration of the people who are to benefit from the estate. What are their needs? What are the planner's aspirations—the benefits he earnestly wants them to enjoy—for them?

It makes little sense to leave a bed-ridden invalid your favorite sports car, guaranteed to get to 110 miles per hour from a standing start in eleven seconds. He can't fold himself into the car, take it out on the highway, or hold it when it corners perfectly at 90. To him the car is either sentimental garbage or a commodity of limited marketability that must be sold for cash. Why not give him cash or income-producing securities instead? Or your wristwatch, which he can use and value sentimentally at the same time?

If that example seems absurd, what about the man who was devoted to a wife of no business experience whatever—and left her solely dependent on a business requiring close personal supervision? Or the chap who accumulated little but earned much and based a family's home and needs on that earning capacity? His legacy is one of property requiring large expenditures to maintain it, tastes requiring large incomes to satisfy them—and no cash to implement either.

The people to be considered in the planning process are *always*:

> The estate owner himself
> His spouse
> His children

As an estate owner's wealth and responsibilities increase, the number of people he is able to consider increases also—and the intimacy of their relationship to him decreases. The list might expand along these lines:

> Parents
> Children-in-law
> Grandchildren
> Brothers and sisters
> Collateral relatives
> Business associates and employees
> Servants
> Friends
> Charities

The list begins with the estate owner himself because he is the first person dependent upon the estate and the first life to be influenced by it. It continues by inclusion of those legally dependent upon him for support and preparation for life and passes on to provision for those morally or sentimentally eligible for benefits.

In determining the needs of beneficiaries one must take into account certain basic considerations, such as health, age, competency, training for self-support and duly established standards of living. Allowances must and can be made for the reduced needs accompanying old age, the completion of education and training for self-support, and the cessation of expenses required by the estate owner's active participation in business or professional life—a circumstance that tends to increase the lavishness of his family spending. Certain fixed and entirely essential commitments will require continuance of the full scale of expenditure, as in cases of severe disability or invalidism. The need for short-term funds for education and vocational or professional training must be considered. Fixed commitments arising out of such items of property as expensive homes, landed estates, etc., must be provided or orderly liquidation of the property arranged.

Part of the process of fixing needs is determining the *form* they will take. In one instance, we may find a need for lifetime income; in another, for aid over a trying but limited period, such as childhood or minority; in yet another, for the satisfaction of a specific and nonrecurring purpose, such as completion of higher education or establishment in another vocation. An approach to planning that begins with people concerns the underlying forces that give direction to their lives. Not only does one consider people as they happen to be, but—in the case of the planner and his immediate family—what they *can* be with adequate self-planning and training.

Only in the rarest cases has it ever been possible for a retired or deceased estate builder to provide enough income from the estate itself to enable his family to continue their previous scale of living without modification. The most important single reason for this used to be that a great capital asset—the man himself—was no longer producing. The only remaining productive force was the estate property. Of late years, this economic truth has been emphasized by the high income taxes and modest interest rates that have made capital accumulation tremendously difficult. As a result, the need for careful planning in all stages of an estate from the first creative steps to the final distribution—even to the planning of the people to whom distribution will be made—has become more vital than ever before.

This business of "planning" the people who will receive an estate means simply training them in the use and production of wealth (a comparative term that applies equally to wage-earner's savings and to great fortunes) and acquainting them with the nature and extent of what they will have so that they will know what they must do.

While the principle may be applied universally, the way it applies will differ sharply in varying circumstances. Its applications will range from instruction in the management of endowed income or substantial capital sums to planning for a self-supporting productive employment. One man might loan his wife funds to invest on her sole responsibility, thus to learn the techniques of management in the school of experience; another might persuade her to study and qualify herself for some kind of job from secretarial through professional—depending upon the abilities and financial resources of the people involved. And children, too, must be trained with an eye on their native abilities and the resources available for them. The boys of one of America's wealthiest families were taught the social responsibilities of wealth and groomed to play the dual role of philanthropist and custodian of huge property interests. Parents who can provide for the long years of study and preparation that come before earnings are realized may encourage gifted children to become doctors, lawyers, engineers, artists. They can plan to that end. Other, less wealthy, parents may have to think in terms of vocational training to give their children trades, or skills at which they can become self-supporting more quickly.

CHAPTER III

DETERMINING NEEDS

Once we get beyond the lowest level of subsistence calculated to just maintain life and minimum health, needs are entirely relative, except when disease or invalidism produce special requirements. It is habit, occasioned and fóstered by living standards adhered to over a long period of years, that determines the extra needs of one person over those of others of like age, physical condition and occupation.

The logical starting point for the determination of needs is an appraisal of present living standards. This requires sharp, careful discrimination between the *family* living standard and that of the individual. Family living standards are often dictated by pressures on the head of the family to maintain a given level of display, to entertain more or less extensively, to be seen at certain places at the proper time. These elements increase the cost and the pace of family living, but have relatively little effect on the scale of the individual. For instance, if we assume a family that has always enjoyed about the same economic standard and that is required by a change in the occupation of the family head to entertain lavishly and to travel extensively, it is probable that the number and variety of clothes in the wardrobe of the individual would be increased and that the quantities of food and liquors—and probably their variety as well—would also be increased. But it is reasonable to assume that the quality of the garments and of the food consumed would not improve. In this instance we would have a definite increase in the family scale of expenditure, with no corresponding increase in the standard of living of the individual members of the family group.

The example could be extended further in that such a family unit could conceivably require a larger home in which to entertain, but the probabilities are that the quality, neighborhood, appointments and services would not be altered. This is important, because it means that a reduction in family expenditures, caused by cessation of the activity that required them, does not necessarily require a corresponding reduction in the standard of living. It is possible for a family group to maintain its accustomed standard of living after the retirement of the head of the family from active business, though on a much smaller budget. Such automatic reduction in family living costs must be borne in mind when the requirements of the estate owner after retirement, or of his dependents after his death, are being evaluated.

The second important factor in the determination of the needs of individuals is that needs vary, even though the same standard of living be maintained, with the age and activity of the person under consideration. In most cases, people tend to develop fixed modes of life as they grow older, and ordinarily live more quietly and on a lower scale of expenditure than in their middle years.

A ready rule-of-thumb for determining income needs may be taken from industry. Most industrial pension plans establish retirement benefits that range from 40% through 60% of the average peak income of the employee. Thus, we may safely determine the income requirements of the individual estate beneficiaries by taking these steps: (1) set down the family expenditures as a whole; (2) subtract the total personal expenditures based upon and required by the business activity of the head of the family; (3) reduce the remainder by that portion of income that represents investment and savings; and (4) accept 40 to 60% of the result as the approximate minimum income need if the accustomed standard of living is to be maintained. Of course, figuring on this basis is figuring on absolute minimum requirements for the maintenance of any given standard. Such planning leaves little leeway, if any; and, therefore, provision must be made or sought for the many kinds of emergencies that might arise in the future. To manage on this basis requires careful thought as to what expenditures are or are not desirable and necessary. But it does not require the sacrifice of quality, nor any serious reduction in the quantity of the things normally consumed by the individual—except in periods of marked inflation, or under other circumstances entirely beyond the control of the planner.

So far we have dealt generally with the evaluation of the needs of individuals dependent upon the estate. Previously we listed the various persons who might have some claim, whether legal or moral, to benefit from the estate. Perhaps this is as good a point as any at which to state flatly that, in all estates but the largest, benefits must be selectively given. The degree and kind of selectivity used, of course, depend upon the personal philosophy of the estate owner; but a reasonable guide may be found in state laws defining one's legal responsibility for support and maintenance and safeguarding the property rights of the kin of a deceased.

Legal responsibility for support and maintenance usually terminates with death. In most jurisdictions, it runs first to the spouse, then to the children, and only after that to the parents, grandchildren and collateral relatives. In New York State, it is confined to two generations either way and to relatives by blood or adoption only. Similarly, most statutes of descent and distribution make effective provision for the spouse and children, even to the point of giving the former well-defined rights to take against the will. Common law states offer protection of the spouse's property rights through dower and curtesy interests. Community property states protect the spouse by giving ownership and power of disposition at death over one-half of the property acquired, other than by gift or inheritance, during marriage.

If the estate is inadequate to provide bountifully for the support of all dependents, it seems logical to start planning with one's spouse and to provide as fully for her needs as possible. It is much more natural for a parent to assume responsibility for the maintenance, education, happiness and comfort of children than for the children voluntarily to assume the same degree of responsibility and consideration for their parents. Therefore, as complete provision as possible for a spouse will usually result in the maximum of benefits, if they be at all deserving, to the children.

But partial provision for the requirements of a spouse and partial provision for one's children is apt to result in an incomplete job from all points of view—and in a good deal of human misery and unhappiness to boot. In these days of extremely high taxes and very limited opportunities for the creation or transmission of substantial estates, more and more people are taking the point of view that the spouse is owed—morally as well as legally—the utmost protection that can be afforded. They feel that the children are moral creditors for no more than as good a start in terms of background, education, training and inculcated virtue and character as it is possible for the parents to give them.

Estate planning is no longer a game concerned with the founding of economic or social dynasties. It is the far more serious business of providing, under the remaining principles of a free economy, independence and self-respect for an estate owner and his dependents. It is seriously concerned with realities and not with the hopeless aspirations of a day-dreamer. That is why we start our planning by urging the complete discharge of moral and legal responsibilities towards the people first entitled to consideration, before even attempting to benefit those having little claim on the planner's assets or sensibilities.

Many of the needs for which provision will be sought are temporary—e.g., maintenance of a larger or more elaborate home than will ultimately be required, provision of maintenance for the few remaining years of life of an extremely elderly person, completion of the amortization or repayment of a mortgage indebtedness upon a home that will be retained and used, and a variety of others. Likewise, there will be some special needs that are not subject to evaluation on the basis of the previously described formula. Such needs may well include the special provision that must be made for an invalid, an incompetent, someone whose benefits must be figured in terms of foreign exchange, or a person so advanced in years . . . and so attuned to a given way of life . . . as to make adjustments completely impossible.

CHAPTER IV

EVALUATING REQUIREMENTS
AND PLANNING PEOPLE

Only the very rich or the entirely poor can plan an estate effectively by merely allocating and arranging assets. The very rich can do so because of the abundance of material they have to work with; the entirely poor because, whatever they do, the end result is always the same—the personal drudgery of their dependents or a reliance upon others to supplement the fortune of "plenty of nothin'". In all other cases, the benefits resulting from mere allocation of what one happens to own will bear no reasonable relation to those that can be provided under a plan based upon a more thorough and careful approach.

Most people are in the middle and do possess an estate, even though it is but the potential embodied in their own earning power. They must start in the middle and roll up the perimeter of the estate planning circle on each side—planning both ways to a central objective—by taking inventory of the assets on one hand and of their beneficiaries' needs on the other. Then they will obtain reasonably accurate knowledge of the differential between the needs and the assets available to satisfy them—and estate planning takes the form of carefully filling in the gaps.

This much we know to start with: The last drop of benefit must be extracted from the assets; and the needs and the aspirations the planner seeks to satisfy must be cut to the bone or there will be no satisfactory solution. For most people, estate planning is merely an orderly way to do these things and to assure good results.

We have already made our start on assaying the needs of all the people, including the estate owner himself, who have claim to benefit from the estate. The next step is to ascertain—with reasonable accuracy—the size, nature and *potential* of the estate. That requires a listing of all assets and offsetting liabilities; an estimate of shrinkages occasioned by various taxes and other causes; allowances for the reductions in value of business interests because of the death of an active participant and consequent loss of credit, productive capacity, market, and "going value";

and an estimate of the *income potential* of the estate as a whole both after death and during life. Then consideration must be given to the estate owner's earning power, as it is one of the great potentials which we can probably capitalize and give identity in the estate itself . . . by systematic investment out of income on a balanced plan, and by adequate, sensible use of insurance and annuities.

From this data we can determine which are "dead" assets that must be liquidated or written off; which are immediately marketable and therefore productive of cash to take care of cash needs; and which are productive of income and to what extent. Thus the balance between assets and needs is tested.

In spite of ruthless reduction of aspirations to the beneficiaries' minimum needs, the process often reveals a shortage in the estate assets available for funding benefits. Then only two courses are open: eliminate one or more of the beneficiaries who are lowest on the ladder of claims, or increase assets in some way to bring them into balance with the objectives. After the number of beneficiaries—and the benefits—has been reduced to the minimum, and the estate potential has been fully realized by making up shortages to the fullest possible extent, any remaining gap between assets and needs can be met in only one way: training of beneficiaries in some field of endeavor productive of income.

Whenever income-producing assets are given or left to a beneficiary—except in trust, under the contractual guarantee of a life insurance company, or by some similar arrangement—it is essential that the recipient be taught something about investment and the management of property. Even though willing reliance upon competent professional advice be characteristic of the beneficiary—knowledge of business, investment, and property management is needed to enable intelligent selection of choices between suggested programs, or intelligent rejection of attractive speculations that may be unsound for the particular purposes of the individual. This is true because an estate is a living thing—even after the death of the original owner—and must be constantly adapted to changing economic conditions and the changing circumstances of the beneficiaries. Neither type of change can be foreseen with certainty and beyond chance of error, so there can be no substitute for trained intelligence on the beneficiary's part. Even though the trust and contract devices (discussed in a later chapter) serve effectively to relieve beneficiaries of administrative detail and worry, they should rarely be so tightly drawn as to bar or hinder adjustment to marked change in economic conditions or personal circumstances.

The type of training given a beneficiary must depend largely on two factors: (1) the ability of the trainee and (2) the economic forecast of the estate owner. Briefly, the training indicated for the beneficiary of the modest estate would be in self-maintenance and useful work; that for beneficiaries of very large estates—to the extent of the individual's capacity to absorb it—would be in the management, conservation, and creation of capital. Since the discharge of full responsibility to the estate owner's surviving spouse is the primary responsibility and, in most cases, requires use of the bulk of the estate, the extent of planning for the future of children is usually limited to provision for the completion of education, and also . . . sometimes . . . of a modest stake to enable a start in life. Education need not—in the greatest number of cases, should not—mean professional training or even university education. It should be gauged to the abilities of the child and the circumstances of the family, so that completion of the program can be reasonably certain. It may well be vocational or business training. At all events, every effort must be made to select a field of endeavor that will produce not only a livelihood, but a happy and well adjusted person.

CHAPTER V

APPRAISING THE ESTATE: ANALYSIS

What we have accomplished in the preceding two chapters was largely a listing and evaluation of the liabilities that we would like to impose on the estate and that we would like it to discharge. To achieve some measure of balance—and to test the practical limitations placed upon us—we must now list and try to evaluate the items on the credit side of the ledger.

Valuations differ with the purpose for which they are made. In this chapter, we are dealing primarily with evaluation for planning purposes, not for tax purposes. The latter could easily take a higher or lower figure, depending on circumstances.

An estate is composed of many items and types of property. It includes all of the property and rights in property of the estate owner whether real or personal.[1] Some of the assets will vanish at the retirement or death of the owner. That one very large capital asset—the earning power of the estate owner himself— will disappear entirely. Several other forms of property, such as life tenancies in trusts, real estate or other estates, may also evaporate at death. Despite the disappearance of this latter group from the estate, there are many instances in which property of this kind serves to increase the taxable estate and so to deplete the estate available for the discharge or satisfaction of the needs discussed previously. This may very well occur when the deceased is one of the life tenants in a trust established by another . . . is given the right to designate a successor or appointee . . . and consequently incurs an added estate tax liability[2] which must be met out of the other assets of his estate and which thus reduces, temporarily at least,[3] the amount available for the discharge of other needs and benefactions. It may occur when the deceased has enjoyed, even though *not used,* the right to invade principal of the trust.[4]

---

[1] *IRC* 1954 §2033; *Reg.* §20.2033.
[2] *IRC* 1954 §2041; *Reg.* §20.2041.
[3] *IRC* 1954 §§2206-7; *Reg.* §20.2205-1.
[4] *IRC* 1954 §2034; *Reg.* §20.2034.

Ordinarily, an estate will consist of items substantially like these:

Personal effects, such as;
> household furnishings
> wearing apparel
> jewelry
> automobiles
> books
> art objects and assorted trivia
> a home
> an interest in a business—close
> corporation, partnership or sole
> proprietorship
> life insurance, including Government
> and National Service policies
> annuities
> cash in checking accounts, savings
> accounts, savings and loan associations
> stocks and bonds.

Additional possibilities are:
> notes
> claims on others
> interests in screwy business ventures
> mortgages
> fees or commissions contingent upon
> completion of a definite task
> accounts in pension or profit-sharing
> plans
> isolated items due from federal agencies
> Social Security benefits, veterans'
> benefits, tax refunds, etc.
> real estate
> interests in trusts or other estates
> other assorted cats and dogs.

The business of evaluating the assets of an estate can present some huge problems. Let us examine the items listed with an eye to appraising their value at the death of the estate-owner.

(1) Personal effects, in most cases, will present no particular

valuation problem. But, if valuable art objects are included amongst them, it is important to realize that, while the value may be very great and may remain quite constant, the market is subject to vagaries and the objects cannot be disposed of unless and until someone of similar taste and means is found. This may involve a long, long wait. If disposition must be made by the executor, he may be faced with a dilemma: the choice between immediate sale for a sum well below true value, or retention beyond the time when the final estate tax return must be filed, (on the chance of finding a more favorable market) with the consequent imposition of a very high tax. If specific disposition is made by will, the executor has no choice but to pay the tax imposed, based on the true value or near it. He will get little consolation from his duty (in absence of a contrary provision) to try to collect the estate tax attributable to the legacy from the legatee. He'll probably have to wait; the property is no easier for the legatee to liquidate than it is for the executor.

(2) A home offers a problem both at retirement and at death. It may be far too large and too elaborate for maintenance after either event. Its true liquidation value is probably far less than its cost—and will be less still when sale is a pressing necessity. Then, too, it may not be readily saleable, because it was designed for the particular needs of a particular family, or because of a change in the character of the neighborhood.

(3) Business interests require thoughtful appraisal. If the interest is one in a comparatively small and closely held business, the chances are one hundred to one that upon retirement or death, a large part of the going value of the business will be sacrificed. The market for the interest is extremely limited and is logically to be found among the persons now connected with, dependent upon, or equitably interested in the business itself. A partnership or closed corporation interest presents a liquidation problem because only the other partners or stockholders would logically be interested in acquiring it. Provision must be made to enable them to pay for it, not only in satisfactory amount but also in a satisfactorily brief time after death or retirement, since payment in small dribs and drabs could go far toward defeating the estate planner's objectives. The state of a sole pro-

prietorship is even worse because, at the moment of death or retirement of the proprietor, virtually the entire going value of the business ceases. What is left is liquidation value, a figure that could be anywhere from 30% to 90% *less* than the going value. Here the problem is to arrange a market for the business at its going value, in order to prevent the otherwise huge estate shrinkage. In most cases, this market must be created by the sole proprietor. In all these instances, a fair evaluation of the business interest in the estate will depend in large part upon the arrangements made for its disposition and upon the funding of those arrangements to guarantee performance.

(4) Life insurance has two values that must be considered in evaluating the estate: the face value of the insurance itself, and the value of the income rights which are part of the insurance contract.

(5) Cash on hand presents no evaluation problem.

(6) Stocks and bonds can be evaluated roughly at their average bid prices or market value over a period of time.

(7) Real estate usually presents a valuation problem since its market value—based on a capitalization of earnings if it be income-producing, or upon average, recent prices for comparable neighboring properties—often deviates widely from its assessed value. Frequently it is a frozen asset—more frequently an asset disposable only at a price unsatisfactory to the heirs—because no buyer will pay more than conservative capitalization, and that price cannot usually be reinvested at the same level of income production.

(8) Interests in trusts or other estates may be difficult to evaluate for planning purposes, especially if they are subject to intervening life interests, or to any other contingencies that cannot be definitely scheduled in time. What weight can or should one give to an income right that may materialize in one year or not for thirty? Yet some weight must be assigned to such deferred but indefeasible interests, since they will be valued and taxed, and so will serve to reduce the values actually on hand—at least until reimbursement of the tax is obtained from the particular trust or estate involved.

We can get a fair idea of the net fortune available—for distribution and allocation to the needs previously determined—by toting up the values listed so far and deducting from their total the aggregate of debts, claims against the estate, administration expenses, and total death and succession taxes. The net figure will probably be a surprise, since it will show the tendency of values to evaporate, even though they have been previously thought of as established. Nevertheless, that net figure is the foundation upon which to base some plan for the creation and maintenance of the additional values actually needed to meet our previously determined needs.

Then, too, because debts, claims and taxes must be paid in cash within a reasonable time—federal estate taxes are due nine months after death—liquidation of assets may have to take place in a poor market. At best, some of the assets will have to be sold somewhat below peak prices. So it is wise to compare values obtainable today, under current conditions and in present day markets, with possible future values or death values.

Often, because of the lower tax rate paid by the new owner, a substantial saving in family income taxes results out of a lifetime transfer that serves to reallocate income within the family group. A 20% reduction in tax is not unusual when a parent shifts income out of his 40% bracket to his child and can save the family $600 yearly on a $3,000 income item. Over a twenty-five-year life expectancy that's $15,000 in added purchasing power!

It is also wise to compare the effect of transfer at death—and the resultant depletion of then values by estate tax—with transfers made during life which are subject to gift tax only upon the values given (assuming that the date of gift is more than three years before the date of death of the donor). It might be revealing to test the death transfer itself against the result of a gift in the amount of the net property that would be transferred after estate taxes. Because a gift reduces the amount—*i.e.*, the total of property owned at death and the adjusted gifts made during life —ultimately subject to tax by the sum of the $3,000 per donee per year exclusions from taxable gifts allowed each donor, the total gift taxes actually paid and all appreciation in value occurring after the date of gift, the ultimate tax may be assessed at lower percentage rates than would otherwise apply.

Possibly even more could ultimately be transferred to heirs, if that portion of the property retained (the amount that would have gone in estate taxes had no lifetime transfers been made) were invested in a non-refund annuity and part of the income of the annuity used to defray premiums on low cost insurance. The annuity would not be present in the estate at death and would not be subject to tax; the insurance need not be present and, even if it were, would serve to supplement that portion of the estate already transferred, and to increase the total net estate to heirs over what would have been available under any other method of transfer.

The following comparison of the results of present transfer by gift with inheritance of the same proportion of an estate shows that gifts taxable at less than the available unified credit have no impact on total transfer taxes, affect merely the timing or incidence of payment. It fails to show: 1. the concealed impact of appreciation in value of the gift property; 2. the possible increased after-tax income resulting from the gift; 3. the cumulative effects of annual gifts equal to the available exclusions—*e.g.*, $3,000 per donee per year for a single donor, $6,000 for a married couple—which may accumulate tidily over many, many years.

(I) Transfer at death only:

Taxable Estate	$100,000	$250,000	$500,000	$1,000,000
Tentative Federal Estate Tax	23,800	70,800	155,800	345,000
Less Unified Estate Tax Credit	47,000	47,000	47,000	47,000
Federal Estate Tax Payable	-	23,800	108,800	298,800
Net to Heirs	100,000	226,200	391,200	701,200

(II) Gift of top 25% of estate, less estate tax:

Net Estate	$100,000	$250,000	$500,000	$1,000,000
Tentative Federal Estate Tax on Top 25%	6,600	20,000	42,500	97,500
Unified Estate Tax Credit Used	6,600	20,000	42,500	47,000
Net Gift	25,000	62,500	125,000	199,500
Gift Tax After Unified Credit	-	-	-	6,630
Net Estate After Gift	75,000	187,500	375,000	793,870
Total Taxable Transfers	97,000	247,000	497,000	990,370
Tentative Federal Estate Tax	22,960	69,840	154,780	342,044
Credit: a. Gift Tax Paid	-	-	-	6,680
b. Unified Credit	22,960	47,000	47,000	47,000
Federal Estate Tax Payable	-	22,840	107,780	288,364
Total to Heirs	100,000	227,160	392,220	705,006

Notes: 1. The unified credit starts at $30,000 in 1977, increases by $4,000 in each of 1978 and 1979 and by $4,500 in each of 1980 and 1981 to reach $47,000. For deaths in years before 1981, the FET must be increased accordingly. 2. The comparison tables assume one donor and one exclusion and unified credit. A spouse may join in a "gift" so "double up" to permit $6,000 exclusion per donee per year and up to $94,000 unified credit. In the table this is not needed as a single $47,000 credit, is sufficient but for a small nubbin of gift tax in the $1,000,000 estate, and the lower phase-in credits offset gift tax in the two smaller estates, in the $500,000 estate after 1980. But the spouse's joinder is available.

CHECKLISTS OF BENEFICIARIES, PURPOSES, TIME OF NEED AND LIQUIDATION VALUES OF ASSETS

These checklists may be helpful if you want to think specifically of the people you want to benefit, why you want to plan for them and when you want their benefits to be effective.

I. WHO?

First Degree Claims	Names
You	....
Your spouse	....
Your children	....
	....
	....
Incompetents	....
	....

Second Degree Claims

Dependent parents	....
	....
Dependent grandparents	....
	....
Dependent brothers	....
	....
Dependent sisters	....
	....
Dependent grandchildren	....
	....
	....
Dependent children-in-law	....
	....
Dependent step-children	....
	....
	....
Dependent wards	....
	....

Third Degree Claims

Friends	....
	....

Independent relatives   ....
                                      ....
                                      ....
Faithful employees   ....
                                      ....
                                      ....
Business associates   ....
                                      ....
                                      ....
Charities   ....
                                      ....
                                      ....
Schools and colleges   ....
                                      ....
                                      ....
Persons owed moral obligations   ....
                                      ....
                                      ....
Godchildren   ....
                                      ....
The U. S. A.   ....

II. WHY?

To Provide

Income; capital; investment control; position and substance; education; a house; etc.

Notes: ....
....
....

To Protect Against

Infancy, old age; improvidence; weakness of character, body or mind; gullibility; inexperience; economic uncertainty; poor business management.

Notes: ....
....
....

To Give

Full or partial power to dispose of or use income or capital; freedom to venture and increase wealth; freedom from worry for dependents; a simple gift.

Notes: ....
....
....

Miscellaneous

To reward for loyalty and merit, to discharge a duty, to make a sentimental gesture.

Notes: ....
....
....

III. WHEN?

During Life

Taking effect immediately; deferred for a period or upon a contingency unrelated to the donor's life; taking effect immediately on a qualified basis and becoming absolute at a later time unrelated to the donor's life.

Notes: ....
....
....

At Death

Taking effect immediately; postponed to a future time or pending a future happening.

Notes: ....
....
....

IV. LIQUIDITY VALUES OF ASSETS

The cash an experienced professional executor may reasonably expect to get for estate assets—and these figures are based on composite experience over many years—may be figured this way:

Asset	Percentage of Market Value
Cash in bank	100
U. S. accumulation bonds	100
Government bonds	100
Municipals	90
Listed bonds	90
Listed common stocks:	
high-grade investment	85
high-grade speculative	70
Preferred stocks	90
Unlisted bonds:	
high-grade	85
other	60
Unlisted stocks:	
high-grade	80
other	30
Mortgages:	
high-grade	100
low-grade	70
Real estate	Your estimate
Close corporation stock:	
subject to P/S contract	Price stipulated
other	100-30
Partnership interests:	
subject to P/S contract	Price stipulated
other	Liquidated value
Proprietorship interests:	
subject to P/S contract	Price stipulated
other	Liquidated value
Interests in trusts and estates, based on underlying assets	100-30
Personal effects	Your estimate
Life Insurance	100
Annuities	100
Other assets	Your estimate

V. BUSINESS LIQUIDATION VALUES

The market value of a business that is to be liquidated is its liquidation value. Depending upon the nature of the business, the ratio of liquidation value of assets to their book value may reasonably be figured this way:

Assets	Percentage on Market Value
Cash	100
Accounts receivable	85-25
Inventory	100-35
Realty	100-50
Fixtures	50-10
Equipment	75-25

PART II

RAW MATERIALS OF PLANNING

CHAPTER VI

THE ECONOMICS OF INVESTMENT — BALANCE

As we use it here, "investment" means the use of capital for the production of income. It is a term that arbitrarily signifies primary concern with security of principal and production of a safe and reasonable income yield. It is used in opposition to "speculative investment" by which we mean the investments made, usually in the initial stages of the creation of an estate, for the purpose of realizing appreciations in value.

If the two basic objectives of investment are security of capital and production of income, periods of inflation and deflation— boom and bust—must both be taken into account to assure a uniform and uninterrupted income flow. This requires the application of the principles of balance to investment, and establishes as the ideal an approximately equal distribution of assets between fixed dollar obligations and so-called equity or ownership assets. In most instances, balance is a principle applicable only to moderately substantial estates; and its application differs greatly as to method at the various stages of the creation of the estate.

During the early years, most of the assets of an estate owner who is actively engaged in a business enterprise in which he has a proprietary interest are apt to be of the equity or ownership type. They are represented by his capital investment in the business itself and by the element of wages for personal activity included in the returns from that business. At this stage of the estate's development, the principle of balance is most closely adhered to by the annual investment of returns of capital or income surpluses in fixed dollar obligations, until an equality of holdings is attained. After disposition of the business interest—either at the retirement or death of the estate owner—emphasis should shift, and the point of balance might well be moved so that a maximum of 30 to 50% of the estate is invested in equity type investments to serve as a hedge against the depreciated purchasing power of the fixed dollar assets in times of price inflation. The change of emphasis is mostly based upon the primary need of dependent beneficiaries for income, and the consequent added importance to them of conservative, non-speculative investment.

A wage or salary earner whose entire income is produced by his own efforts and is based largely upon a tight-knit accumulation of energy, skills, and habits is in precisely the same position as the man who has invested in a business. The only difference is that the total capital of the wage or salary earner is invested in himself and thus has no separate economic existence. It is, nevertheless, an equity or ownership asset, because returns upon the investment are based entirely upon earnings, and are not fixed and subject to payment without regard to the profits of the obligor in any given period. This man's problem is to create an estate—a separate economic entity that is independent of his own productive employment—in a form so well-balanced that it will take care of his needs and those of his dependents during all stages of the economic cycle.

The problem of balancing the investments of a personal estate divides into two major parts: The first is concerned with creating balanced investment during life; the second with providing a balanced portfolio after death for the maintenance of those then dependent upon it. During life, the deflationary hedge can be efficiently created by the use of annuities and life insurance that may be purchased and will be paid out over a long period of time and, therefore, in dollars of average purchasing power. After death, the same insurance investments will stand in similar relation to dependents. They will assure an underlying fixed dollar income base that is almost always tremendously enlarged, because death causes the insurance to ripen into its full indemnity value. Then the other property of the estate may be used to hedge the inflationary periods to come.

In order to simplify the application of the principle of balance, we have arbitrarily classified investment into three general categories: investment reflecting earnings, fixed dollar investment, and non-income counter-inflationary investment.

The first group—investment reflecting earnings—includes:
>   common stock
>   preferred stock inadequately secured
>   bonds inadequately secured
>   business or partnership interests
>   first mortgages inadequately secured
>   second or third mortgages
>   royalties
>   salary or wages
>   balances in employee profit-sharing trust plans.

The second group—fixed dollar investment—includes:
>   bonds adequately secured
>   first mortgages adequately secured
>   preferred stock adequately secured
>   bank accounts
>   insurance maturity values
>   balances in employee pension trust plans
>   veterans' or other cash or income benefits
>   Social Security benefits.

The third group—non-income counter-inflationary investment
—includes:
>   real estate held for personal use
>   real estate held for appreciation—vacant land
>   tangible personalty such as jewelry, art objects,
>   furnishings, etc.

An important thing to remember, and one which is most commonly overlooked, is that all capital is of two kinds or, more properly, is found in two forms: capital already invested and capital annually available for investment. It is no problem to distinguish between these two in those cases in which accumulated, already invested wealth produces annual sums which are both a return *on* the invested capital and a return *of* the invested capital, occasioned by amortizations or maturities. It is no less important, however, to realize that the annual flow of money which results from the efforts and labor of the salary or wage earner also represents income *and a return of capital.* Just as surely as a prudent businessman arranges for the depreciation and amortization of the value of equipment used in the production of goods, so should the wage or salary earner arrange for the prudent amortization of his capital value. The investment of a reasonable proportion of the annual return of capital in fixed dollar obligations—to offset the total equity investment represented by the man himself—is a basic and fundamental application of the principle of balance. The utilization of self-liquidating investment, which will be discussed in the succeeding chapter, will enable skillful preservation of balanced investment, both during the life of the estate owner and after his death.

CHAPTER VII

SELF-LIQUIDATING INVESTMENT

For hundreds of years, wealth in England has been measured in terms of income. In the United States, still a relatively young country, its measure until the past few years has been in terms of total accumulation or capital. Presumably, the major reason for this difference in concept is that until quite recently, the opportunity for capital accumulation and growth in the United States was outstanding and subject only to personal limitations of acumen, energy, industry; while in England, no new frontiers remained for conquest. There a caste system, which had developed under feudalism, carried on throughout the industrial life of the nation. Together with the principles of entailed wealth and inheritance by the oldest son, which persisted in the social system, it served to limit severely opportunities for accumulation of wealth, and the establishment of new personal fortunes.

So, realistically, the entire British concept of wealth became one of available income; since it was the income on already accumulated inherited capital, rather than comparatively easily won capital additions, that determined the standard of living. It was perfectly logical that this economic stability and its attendant attitude of mind should result in a wide acceptance and use of annuities, because only the principle of self-liquidating investment makes it possible to raise a standard of living when increases in capital accumulation are extremely difficult, if not impossible.

The practicality and appeal of self-liquidating investment are based on two fundamental concepts: (1) the paramount need for income, since accumulations of capital as such are worthless, except to the extent that they produce spendable and reasonably assured income on some continuous basis; and (2) the fact that the basic need to keep income-producing capital funds intact is eliminated, once some other system is found to guarantee distribution of income and installments of capital over any predetermined period, whatever the duration. The great appeal of an asset that consumes itself but always lasts out the period for which it is needed is: Considerably less capital is required to finance any specific scale of living when both capital and interest may be distributed over the required period, than when a capital fund must be held intact in order to guarantee continuance of income at the relatively low rate available when due consideration is given to security of principal.

It seems apparent that the basic reason for the popularity and widespread acceptance of the self-liquidating investment in the British economy was the limitation upon large new capital accumulations. The startling fact, though, is that the same limitation has developed with amazing rapidity in the American economy . . . but for vastly different reasons. In America, the backwash of the Industrial Revolution, and the waves of recession sweeping over the country from Europe, created a period of marked deflation commencing about 1929 and continuing with little or no interruption until 1941. In the wake of this wave of world-wide recession came the passionate and articulate demand of the people for security—for some assurance of the provision by government of those things which they were helpless to accomplish for themselves as individuals in the face of the world-wide economic limitations engulfing the country.

Totally apart from the question of the soundness of the economic approach, there can be little dispute as to the fact that humanitarian reasons compelled the provision of additional government services, insurances, and monies for the relief of need and the alleviation of unemployment. The result was an inevitable and spectacular rise in the cost of government. Concurrently, money rates sank virtually to zero because of the very unattractive possibilities for invested capital. Much of the deficit spending of the government was arranged on loans—obtained, in the earlier days of the program, from banks, insurance companies, and industrial corporations—at the lowest possible rate of interest. Continued borrowing by government at low interest rates tended to continue the depressed condition of money rates. Hence, it was almost impossible, for twenty odd years beginning in the middle 1930's, to accumulate money or to invest capital at a rate of interest approaching, much less exceeding, 3% per annum.

In addition to depressed interest rates, increased government costs—totally aside from any special war costs—mounted so rapidly and to such a height that the increase in the effective income tax rate is startling. In 1932, a married man with one child paid $4.00 in federal income tax on an income of $3,000, $124 on an income of $6,000; in 1947, he had to pay $307 on the $3,000 income and $1,165 on the income of $6,000. In 1948, income-splitting came along, helping somewhat—the $3,000 income called for $153 tax and the $6,000 income for $598; but, in 1952, the bill went up once again to $185 and $740 on the respective incomes. For the years 1968 through 1970 a surcharge of 7.5% of the tax for 1968, 10% for 1969, and 2½% for 1970 was added to the individual's tax. At its height, that brought the tax to $203.50 on the $3,000 income and $814 on the $6,000 one. Now, under the Tax Reduction Act of 1977, and its zero bracket amount, no tax lies on the $3,000 income and that on the $6,000 income drops to $77, subject to the $35 credit per exemption. But these reductions have been more than offset by the rapidly rising costs of living resulting from continuing inflationary pressures. At the higher income levels, despite some apparent relief—*e.g.,* limiting the tax on earned income to 50%—additional taxes and eliminations of preferences have intensified the restraints upon accumulation of wealth.

The earning power of money was persistently low—on AAA bonds, for example, from 3.5% to 4½%—until 1966 when yields broke through 5%, eventually reaching about 8% before retreating to their present about 7% level. That tended to complicate accumulations of wealth out of personal earnings. Combined with high personal tax rates it made the task virtually impossible—and even in light of presently increased yields and modified taxes, high living costs tend to keep it so.

Take as an example the professional man of 40, who should have been able to anticipate another twenty years of productive activity. If we assume him to have had an average net income, after exemptions, of $10,000, we will find his 1947 federal income tax alone came to $2,508; his 1948 tax to $2,304 and his 1952 tax to $2,956. If we assume further that he could and did live on only $5,000—one-half of his net income—and saved the balance, he added $2,044 to his estate each year. After twenty years of earning and saving, his accumulations without interest amounted to $40,880. Invested at 2.5%—the then high yield on government bonds—this estate would yield all of $1,022 annually. Patently there was no solution for this man's problem other than to turn to self-liquidating investment. He is in precisely the same position as his British cousin: It matters little what he has in the bank or on the books. Only what he has available to spend and to live upon counts.

But hasn't the situation changed? Isn't today's outlook different?

While interest rates have increased somewhat in the past several years, from the middle and late 1950's to the present, and common stocks have tended to rise in value, the basic situation has not changed. Stock yields in terms of market prices discounting twenty to thirty years' earnings are still modest. Perhaps a well-diversified portfolio can show an average 3.67 to 4.50%, but not without risk. And lack of diversification multiplies the risk enormously. Bonds now will yield 5% to 7¼% and savings banks and savings and loan associations 5% to 6%, but the effect upon total accumulations is watered down by earlier lower yields and history shows that the short-run swings from low to high and back again make a lifetime average of 3% very good indeed. An average of 2.5% is high—especially when losses as well as gains are counted on the record.

And another factor has developed to complicate the problem. Living costs have increased spectacularly during the boom or inflationary years.

Still the only medium in which one can be sure of accumulating sufficient capital to supplant personal earnings is one having these elements:

(1) The highest possible rate of guaranteed accumulation upon past and current deposits;

(2) The deferral of income taxes on that accumulation in order to derive full benefit from the compounding of interest upon interest; and

(3) The availability of the annuity principle at no cost in addition to the original cost of investment, so that capital and income can be drawn down systematically over a lifetime—which is utilization of the principle of self-liquidating investment.

CHAPTER VIII

SELECTION OF PROPERTY FORMS

One essential of estate planning is the selection of the forms of property to be transferred to ultimate heirs or to be retained by the estate owner through his retirement. Even though the heirs and the estate owner himself will have to rely upon the income produced by the estate, there is usually no planned or deliberate selection of property forms. Most often, the estate is an accumulation of odd lots of flotsam and jetsam—acquired without plan, correlation or visualization of results—during a lifetime of part time investment. It is the result of an indifferent and undiscriminating acceptance of "tips" and amateur counsel.

But sometime the estate owner must take responsibility for the selection of the property to be acquired or retained in his portfolio. Failure to do so may end in a decided estate inadequacy—insufficient income yield. It almost always produces unnecessary reinvestment problems, management and administrative worries and a host of both minor and major annoyances. Such a picture is bad enough during retirement and while the estate owner is still alive. After his death it may turn into sheer chaos and result in bequests of problems, delays and eventual financial insufficiency, instead of the benefits he sought to bestow.

We have spoken previously of the need for a change of emphasis at the end of the period of accumulation, when the estate owner's primary requirement becomes assured income. This transfer of emphasis usually involves a change in the forms and specific pieces of property held in the portfolio. It requires cautious selection of property forms adapted to and consistent with the need and the purposes to which the property and its product will be put.

The principal objectives of such a change in portfolio are: (1) lesser emphasis upon equity assets of the type requiring either personal participation in the income-producing activity, or close and detailed management supervision; (2) drastic reduction in the emphasis placed upon assets held primarily for capital appreciation; (3) increased emphasis upon assets held for the production of income, either on the basis of principal kept intact for future distribution to others, or on the basis of self-liquidating investment, with or without survivorship provisions; (4) careful consideration of the wisdom of liquidating non-income-producing assets that are at the same time income-consuming—such as elaborate homes or large landed estates.

Selection of property forms for one's heirs requires even more discrimination. The imposition of heavy taxes upon transfers to heirs requires large cash resources or high liquidity of a relatively large portion of the assets subject to transfer, if a shocking degree of shrinkage resulting from forced sale is to be avoided. The basis of a proper selection of property forms for ultimate heirs is, therefore, the dual one of the needs of the people who will be dependent upon the property and the needs of the estate itself for cash for the payment of the required transfer costs and death duties. To this end, we can arbitrarily classify assets into those:

(a) Producing income but frozen as to capital value, such as: large real estate holdings in urban areas, farms actually in production, interests in business ventures other than those listed upon national Stock Exchanges.

(b) Producing no income but essentially liquid as to capital value, such as: cash on hand, jewels, negotiable and marketable but non-interest-bearing promissory notes, remainder interests, interests in trusts and other estates and cash claims against others;

(c) Producing income and more or less liquid as to capital, such as: liquid stocks and bonds, insurance policies, annuity remainders or survivorship interests, Social Security and United States Government veterans' income benefits.

(d) Producing non-economic satisfactions but lacking in income value and frozen as to capital, such as: fine books, art objects, house furnishings, vacant land and other forms of property enjoying only a limited market.

The administrative expense of an average, moderately substantial estate may be safely assumed to be 5%. It may run more in smaller estates and perhaps somewhat less in the very much larger ones. Federal transfer taxes actually payable after application of the available unified credit for estate taxes will reach somwhere between 30% and 70% of the estate in excess of the $175,625 as to which the $47,000 credit will completely offset tax. [The comparable "exempt" amounts when death occurs before 1981 are: $120,000 in 1977 (credit $30,000); $134,000 in 1978 (credit $34,000); $147,000 in 1979 (credit $38,000); $162,000 in 1980 (credit $42,500).] Additional shrinkages, usually large in proportion, will occur as a result of prevailing distress conditions or of the possible limited saleability of property that must be liquidated in order to realize the cash required for taxes, administration, cash bequests, and funeral and medical expenses. From the standpoint of the needs of the estate itself, then, due consideration must be given to the requirement of liquidity of assets, or the maintenance of an adequate cash fund.

When planning to satisfy needs of the heirs, care must be exercised to prevent confusion of the over-all appraised value of the assets with their actual value in terms of meeting the income and cash requirements of the beneficiaries. It matters very little to beneficiaries who need $50 a week that the over-all value of an estate is $350,000, if that $350,000 is represented by a Rubens Madonna which can be disposed of only to a handful of million-aire collectors or to a museum. The Madonna will not produce $50 a week. However, she will produce an interesting and gorgeous estate tax liability. Let's grant that that is a *reductio ad absurdum.* It is still an altogether too frequent occurrence in many estates.

From the standpoint of estate planning to provide for the needs of the beneficiaries, it is wise to liquidate those objects of beauty and value that serve primarily to satisfy our possessive instincts and to substitute for them property of greater invest-ment utility. Once again, the touchstone should be the British standard of "What will this be worth in terms of annual income?" not the American standard of "What is the repre-sentative capital value of this property? " To plan for the satisfaction of the needs of heirs, we must think of the estate assets in terms of their present market value and the translation of that market value into income at present market yield. Often we must go farther still and actually follow through the process—

disposing of the Rubens Madonna, the landed estates, the Shakespeare Quartos, and the stock in that business Joe Smith started fifteen years ago and that you just know will be worth a hundred thousand dollars before his great-grandchildren are dead.

The process of estate planning requires first of all that the estate planner stop lying to himself, stop looking at things as they might be, and take stock of them as they actually are. Secondly, the process requires that he utilize things as they are for the purpose of changing them over into what they reasonably can be. To leave this task to heirs or beneficiaries is the ultimate in shirking responsibility. To undertake it oneself is to make possible—by the judicious use of self-liquidating investments and thoughtful changes in the existing portfolio—the complete satisfaction of income requirements that at first appear well beyond the capacities of the estate being planned. We must start, therefore, not with the concept of the estate as it is; but with a knowledge of the value of the estate and a concept of what that value could accomplish.

CHAPTER IX

LIVING AND TESTAMENTARY TRANSFERS

Property may be transferred in three basic ways: (1) by sale or transfer for a consideration in money or money's worth; (2) by donation; and (3) by operation of law. While all three methods of transfer are important in estate planning as a whole, it is only the latter two that need be considered—in the ordinary course of things—in planning the *disposition* of an estate.

The persons an estate-owner wishes to benefit may receive the property he wants them to have by gift—a voluntary and gratuitous transfer—or by operation of law or inheritance. Transfers by operation of law occur whenever there is no will or, and more importantly, when the dispositions made by will allot less to certain favored heirs—usually spouse and children—than the minimum given them by law. Such heirs may then "take against the will"—that is, rely upon operation of law for their benefits. Clearly, then, not only the failure to make a will, but also improper advice and the consequent failure of testamentary disposition, may result in transfers by operation of law.

But estate planning is conscious and deliberate, so we shall concern ourselves only with the second category of transfers— donations or gifts. In so doing, we shall examine the possibilities inherent in them, whether made during life or in the form of bequests, which are, after all, simply gifts made by conscious direction during life but becoming effective only at death.

There are many differences between gifts made during life and those made at death. They extend from the obvious . . . such as the time when the gift becomes effective from the viewpoint of the beneficiaries, to the subtle . . . such as the inherent costs of transfer and the degree of sacrifice required of the donor. Most types of gifts are useful, but each has its place, and the decision to adopt one or the other must be based upon several considerations.

One of the considerations to be weighed is that of the personal satisfactions stemming from the act of giving. Some of the factors are intangible, such as the added pleasure the estate owner gets from being able to see the property he has given enjoyed and used as he wanted it to be. So the giver must weigh this kind of satisfaction against his personal sacrifice in terms of lost income or enjoyment. But other things enter into consideration, too, and often are extremely tangible. Gifts during life to employees, children, or members of the family who would ordinarily inherit the property, may carry with them tangible and material benefits, as well as merely added satisfaction and enjoyment.

For instance, employees may function more happily and more efficiently because of a present gift of a business interest which they would ordinarily receive only after the death of the employer; distribution of property to members of one's family may not result in any net reduction in enjoyment because the economic benefits might still be available to all members of a close-knit family group; and, finally, the income receivable by the donor from the property which he is giving away may fall into such a very high personal income tax bracket that his net measure of enjoyment is far outweighed by the satisfaction of giving.

This last situation can arise very easily in the estates of wealthy persons who may find the top portions of their income taxed at anywhere from 70% to 90%. They can benefit others whose interests they hold at heart at a cost of only a 10% to 30% measure of enjoyment to themselves. In other situations, they can relieve themselves of 70% to 90% of the drain imposed by the obligation to pay fixed allowances to others.

Example 1: The top $10,000 of a $60,000 taxable income is taxed at 77%. The gift of property yielding $5,000 annually costs the donor only $1,250 of spendable income.

Example 2: The same property owner becomes obligated to pay a dependent $5,000 annually. He must meet the tax on that sum, so must allocate nearly $22,000 of his income to the purpose. A gift of property yielding $5,000 annually would save him $17,000 before and $3,850 after personal income taxes.

Another set of considerations is that of the costs of transfer and the net effect, upon the estate viewed as a whole, of making transfers during life rather than by will. Although gift tax rates and estate tax rates are the same, the incidence of tax differs and gift taxes start at the bottom of the tax ladder as payments on account of the ultimate unified transfer tax. Taxable gifts are always net of the $3,000 annual exclusion for gifts of present interest made by a donor to each donee each year, and the unified credit for gift taxes applies against the tentative gift tax so that substantial gifts may be made without immediate tax cost —especially when spouses join to double-up, in effect, by applying their individual exclusions and uniform credits to the aggregate gifts made.

Unless gifts are made within three years of the date of the donor's death, any gift tax paid and any annual exclusions allowed escape inclusion in the ultimate transfer tax base. So does any increase in the value of the gift property between the date of gift and the date of death. If the gift is treated as a transfer at death because of some technical error in implementing the gift, only the date of death value is so treated—the gift tax and the exclusions taken are not brought back into the death tax base. So, when a valid gift passes appreciating property to a donee, the sum of the transfer taxes paid on what was not given away and on the amount given during life is apt to be substantially less than the total estate taxes that would have been levied at date of death values had all the property been retained until then.

If this is borne in mind and consideration is given to the effect of high personal income taxes, it is not difficult to see that there can be some situations in which judicious giving during life can result in added benefits to all persons concerned. For instance, the owner of a large estate could give his heirs approximately one-third of his estate, and buy an immediate life annuity with the amount that would have to be paid in estate tax on that third, if it passed by his will. This is what would happen:

First, the heirs would get immediate benefits from the gift and the income produced by it would be taxed in lower personal income tax brackets, thus increasing the total income from the estate as a whole to all recipients. Second, death taxes would necessarily be reduced to a considerable degree since the estate would have been reduced by the amount of the gift, the amount invested in the immediate life annuity, and the actual sum of gift taxes paid. And, third, since the income from the annuity would be largely income tax-free, the donor would find that either the gift had cost him little in terms of income, or that he had actually benefited by increasing the net income left him after the payment of personal taxes.

There is another and subtle distinction in the application of gift taxes and estate taxes. Under the estate tax law not only is the property actually transferred to heirs subject to estate taxes, but so is the estate tax payable upon it. In other words, a $100,000 bequest in a $100,000 estate is valued at $100,000; not at the net amount which the heirs would receive after payment of the estate tax. A gift of $100,000, however, is valued on the basis of the net amount receivable by the donee. If you wish to give $100,000 to someone, you must pay a tax based upon that value; but if you wish only to set aside $100,000 to cover both the gift and the tax, you will pay a tax which is based upon the difference between the total set aside and the amount paid government by way of tax.

The advisability of making gifts during life depends—as do most decisions in estate planning—upon the people and the circumstances involved in the particular estate under consideration. There is no rule which can be postulated to replace thought and the careful weighing of advantages in each instance. There is no magic formula. Nowhere in the entire process of planning an estate can a substitute be devised for thought, technical knowl edge and careful consideration of the basic principles which must be applied to the individual circumstances of each case.

While gifts properly made during life are the most effective way to reduce estate taxes and, in some cases, to reduce current income taxes, with a resultant increase in the net income of the donor, they are not to be casually or easily made. Various factors must be considered and certain definite standards closely adhered to, if gifts are to be effective for tax purposes and economically sound.

Several economic factors are involved.

One of these is the age of the estate owner, as gifts which are designed to save estate tax must necessarily be made in such a way that ownership passes completely and absolutely from the donor to the donee. As a result, the property which is the subject of the gift is forever and irrevocably removed from the possession of the donor and cannot be relied upon or recovered in the event of subsequent reverses or emergencies. Therefore, estate owners of young or middle-age should weigh the making of gifts very carefully indeed, because of the impossibility of predicting accurately enough what their personal financial circumstances are apt to be in the distant future. Then, the tax saving involved in making gifts is merely the amount of estate tax saved on the aggregate of the gift tax paid and the annual exclusions taken. (Transfer taxes saved on value appreciation are ignored because of the impossibility of making reasonable quantitative estimates.)

Estate taxes are not due or payable until nine months after the date of death and gift taxes are payable on February fifteenth of the year following that in which aggregate taxable gifts of $25,000 or less were made; on the fifteenth day of the second month following the end of the calendar quarter in which the unreported taxable gifts for the calendar year exceed $25,000. Hence, to arrive at a true economic valuation of the amount saved, we must weight the gift tax at a given conservative rate of interest for the remaining life expectancy of the donor, on the theory that in reality he has paid a tax that will not normally be due for many years; has lost income on the money given; and must take these factors into account in order to arrive at a true result. Against these possible disadvantages, consideration must be given to the expected appreciation in value of the property given and so eliminated from the estate tax base and to the possible arbitrage in income tax rates resulting from application of the lower effective rates of the donee (trust, child, or other) to the income from the property over the same measuring period. It follows that the true or actual saving may be considerably reduced when a gift is made by a very young man, because of the additional expectation of life remaining to him.

It must also be remembered that certain gifts do not lighten the donor's income tax burden, and others do not reduce his taxable estate one whit. Thus gifts in trust do not produce any income tax benefit when: (1) the income is to be used, and actually is used, for the education, maintenance and support of minor children legally dependent upon the donor; (2) the donor has reserved the income, or it is to be accumulated for possible distribution to him or his spouse; (3) the income is or may be applied to the payment of premiums on insurance on his own life or that of his spouse; or (4) the income is or may be used to discharge his legal obligations. Just so, no estate tax benefit results from gifts made within three years of death, or from gifts which do not finally vest in the possession or enjoyment of the recipient until or after the death of the donor, except that the gift tax paid as to the later will not be drawn into taxable estate; nor will any increase in value attributable to improvements or contributions of the donee—between the date of gift and that of death—be drawn into gross estate.

The character of the assets composing an estate has a very definite bearing upon the advisability of making gifts. If assets are not readily divisible, or convertible into cash with a minimum of loss and cost, the process will be too cumbersome to be worthwhile. One example of this situation is the gift of shares in a close corporation or of an interest in a partnership—potentially very dangerous if the donor deprives himself of control. Another is that of real property which is not easily divisible and the joint ownership of which could become highly uncomfortable if there were any subsequent lack of agreement between the donor and the donee.

While some of the tax considerations for making gifts are more properly treated as economic considerations, there are others that go directly to the root of the matter and have straightforward bearing on whether or not a tax-saving will be effective. One of them, the need for complete and absolute divestment of the donor of all interest in the property, has already been mentioned. The others are largely questions of the motive underlying the gift.

It is, of course, possible to make a gift of the income of property for a term of years without abandoning all rights to the underlying property itself. Under the present law and rules, such a gift of income for not less than ten years may be made in trust and a complete reversionary interest in the underlying trust property may be retained. Properly done, the "term" or "reversionary" trust effectively shifts the impact of income taxes to the donee or trustee; gives rise to a gift tax based on the discounted value of the right to income donated; and has no effect upon the donor's estate tax liability, since the value of his right to recover the trust corpus will be included in his estate. For example, a gift of the income from $10,000 in trust for ten years, after which the donor gets back $10,000, is valued at $4,416—arrived at by subtracting from $10,000 the $5,584 value discounted at 6% of the right to get back $10,000 after ten years.

Once it was necessary to determine whether a gift had been made for motives associated with life or those associated with death. The latter effectively nullified all estate tax benefit sought by the gift. A statutory test was developed to provide some certainty in this otherwise wild card area and took the form of a rebuttable presumption that a transfer made less than three years before death was indeed "in contemplation" and an irrebuttable presumption that any transfer made more than three years before death was not.

The Tax Reform Act of 1976 introduced the unified transfer concept and did away with any contemplation of death concepts or problems. Instead, it merely provides that the date of death value of all property transferred within three years of death and the gift taxes paid upon it are to be included in gross estate for estate tax purposes. Only the amounts excludable in computing taxable gifts—*i.e.,* the $3,000 per year exclusion allowed for each donee—is left unrecaptured.

Gifts in another category—those becoming effective as to the possession or enjoyment of property at or after the death of the donor—are entirely ineffective from the standpoint of estate tax savings. They are included in full in the estate of the donor, despite their irrevocability. Under the current statute, any gift of whatever nature may be so classified if the ultimate assurance of enjoyment by the donees can be related to or made in any way dependent upon the death of the donor. An example is a trust running to named beneficiaries but under which the grantor reserves a power of appointment should he survive all the beneficiaries and their issue. Still another is the trust under which income is to be accumulated for the grantor's life, and both accumulated income and principal are to be distributed to the beneficiaries at the grantor's death. While the grantor could never benefit nor determine who should benefit, the principal of the trust is includable in his gross estate.

8. Elimination of financial care or worry

9. To please one's family

10. To minimize federal income taxes

11. To make up a deficiency in a son's earnings

12. Equalization of children's interests in one's property

13. To reward the constancy or loyalty of employees

Gifts in another category—those becoming effective as to the possession or enjoyment of property at or after the death of the donor—are entirely ineffective from the standpoint of estate tax savings. They are included in full in the estate of the donor, despite their irrevocability. Under the current statute, any gift of whatever nature may be so classified if the ultimate assurance of enjoyment by the donees can be related to or made in any way dependent upon the death of the donor. An example is a trust running to named beneficiaries but under which the grantor reserves a power of appointment should he survive all the beneficiaries and their issue. Still another is the trust under which income is to be accumulated for the grantor's life, and both accumulated income and principal are to be distributed to the beneficiaries at the grantor's death. While the grantor could never benefit nor determine who should benefit, the principal of the trust is includable in his gross estate.

CHAPTER X

PROBLEMS OF ADMINISTRATION

An estate always presents administration problems. The property of the estate must be watched: sums paid on the maturity of investment must be reinvested; assets must be purchased or sold as opportunities to make a profit or avert a loss present themselves. Decisions of many kinds and of varying import must be made in connection with the property of the estate and the rights of the various beneficiaries. Legal action may have to be taken to protect the assets. Proper allocation of sums flowing into the estate as to returns of capital, income and necessary reserves for various purposes must be made on a continuous basis.

During the period of accumulation, the estate owner ordinarily assumes these responsibilities himself. Sometimes he shares them with a bank or trust company through the medium of a custodial account—thus obtaining the services of full time expert investment counsel while retaining the right to make his own ultimate decisions. But, he may be less willing to continue assumption of these responsibilities after retirement. Then, too, he may feel that some or all of those who will benefit from his estate at his death are not competent to perform these tasks. He may decide to make lifetime income provisions for certain people, and give still others whatever funds remain after the death of the income beneficiaries.

Broadly speaking, there are two ways to transfer the burden of management to other shoulders and yet to assure continuity of management over two or more lives. One is the use of trusts placed with a corporate trustee (or with individual trustees if proper precautions are taken to assure successor-trustees in the event of death). The other is contractual investment, obtainable on a modified scale from investment trusts and on a well-developed scale from legal reserve life insurance companies. The trust method permits the use of many kinds of property, the management of which will be assumed by the trustee and performed by him or for him through duly authorized and retained agents.

The contract medium requires the use of cash because it consists, in effect, of purchasing a share in the large and well-diversified investment portfolio of the particular investment or insurance company or companies selected. If the trust is used, the property placed in trust will stand alone and will bear the full impact of any losses that might be sustained—and the full benefit of any profits that might be made. If contractual investment is used, the cash placed with the investment or insurance company will be mingled with the assets of the company, and the over-all profits and losses of the company will be shared proportionately among the individual contract holders. Since proper diversification geographically, by maturities and by items, is difficult to obtain on a well-developed scale—except when large funds are available—safety considerations tend to give added weight to contractual investment.

Both the trust and contract media offer convenient and efficient ways to assure continuity of management for one's beneficiaries and to limit costs of administration to a foreseeable sum. Trustees' fees are moderate and stipulated in the agreement. And trustees are held to strict accountability for their actions, which must be those of a prudent and reasonable man administering as though the assets were his and were to be used for his own best advantage. Both investment and insurance companies are severely regulated by law, and the latter are subject to close supervision of the various state insurance departments. The premium or consideration originally paid for the contract constitutes the only management or administration fee that the insurance company charges.

Both media make it possible to escape liability for estate tax upon the first and second transfers subsequent to the death of the estate owner. Both offer attractive estate conservation opportunities and an efficient mechanism for the payment of income benefits to certain beneficiaries and remainder benefits to others. Both provide continuity of conservative and skilled management at low cost—even though their legal characteristics are very different indeed.

A comparison of the legal characteristics of trusts and contractual investment is not offered because it would be out of place and singularly dull. But a few distinctions should be made because they are important to the estate owner and may affect his planning:

The trustee is not in a position to guarantee capital or any payment of income; he is charged merely with prudent and wise management of the property entrusted to him. He is powerless to make up deficits of income or capital out of other trusts or other funds at his disposal. The insurance company can and does guarantee safety of principal and payment of a minimum rate of income. An insurance company is obliged to make them up out of its own surplus and contingency reserves, which are operated for just that purpose. A trustee may exercise any degree of discretion the grantor of the trust is willing to give him, or the responsibility for which the trustee is willing to accept. The exercise of discretion is quite a common characteristic of trusts and gives them a distinct advantage as to flexibility over the insurance contract. The insurance company—acting as it does entirely under contract—may not exercise or accept a direction to exercise any discretion whatsoever. It will merely carry out precisely the provisions of the contract governing its relationship with the other contracting party. The investment trust—usually a mutual fund or regulated investment company—operates under the limitations of its contract. It cannot guarantee either principal or yield, although losses and gains are allocated proportionately to all shares, since they are absorbed by the total fund. It cannot assume life contingency risks or guarantee the duration of income. It seems to fall between the completely individual vulnerability of the trust and the full guarantees of the insurance company.

Certain definite limitations are placed upon the period for which funds may be held in trust. The old common law—still in effect in many states—established the maximum time for which funds could be "alienated" or suspended in a state short of unfettered ownership at any number of lives in being, plus twenty-one years, plus the period of gestation. In some states, more modern codes set forth specific statutory periods establishing arbitrary limits. While the law is not very clear as to the applicability of such limiting statutes or rules against perpetuities to insurance policies or any other forms of contract, most insurance companies work on the theory that they are subject to the same limitations as trusts, and will not accept a directive to hold funds intact for the production of income for any period conflicting with the statute or rule against perpetuities in the state of contract.

Both the trust and contract media may be made operative in whole or in part during the lifetime of the estate owner, or at and after his death. Property can be placed in trust, either subject to or divorced from the management of the trustor, for his own benefit or for that of others during his lifetime; or it may be placed in a testamentary trust effected by his will and becoming operative only after his death. Contractual arrangements may be made with insurance companies for the payment of income benefits to the estate owner and the continuance of those benefits to his beneficiaries or heirs after his death. Or the contract may call (as does an ordinary contract of life insurance) merely for the guardianship and accumulation of funds during the estate owner's lifetime, and for the function of the company as administrator and conservator in toto, to operate only for the benefit of the insured's heirs and to begin only after his death. Frequently, effective use can be made of a combination of both media; and frequently each of them is used on both a living and a testamentary basis.

It is the use of trust or contract arrangements that results in "avoidance of probate" as to the wealth so arranged. Thus, as to the trust assets, insurance proceeds or other contract benefits there may well be somewhat prompter payment directly to the designated beneficiaries or payees, or a continuance of smooth operation without the interruption caused by the need for administration and—to a degree—without the expense of administration. But *total* avoidance of probate—i.e., of administration—is not possible or desirable. Nor is total avoidance of administration costs possible in most cases.

It's obviously impractical to put one's personal things—e.g., clothes, personal bank accounts, auto, etc.—in trust unless one deludes oneself by a declaration that one is holding them in trust for another. It is impractical because wholly unimpeded use and consumption are necessary to the human condition. It is delusory because such a trust would be ineffective for federal tax purposes as a transfer subject to retention of use and benefit for life, would require a trustee—here's the administration problem!—to wind up and turn over to the beneficiaries and would incur true administration expense or its equivalent since the personal representative (the executor under a will or the administrator if you have no will) would have to "administer" by demanding contribution to any death taxes due and handling the returns, accounting, and monies.

Intelligently used as adjuncts to the will, trust and contract arrangements make marvelously good sense. But they do not serve well alone and the will does not usually operate upon them or upon jointly held property, which is owned under a "sort of" contract deriving from its title provisions.

CHECKLIST OF GIFT POSSIBILITIES — WHAT AND HOW

These checklists may be helpful if you want to think specifically of what you want to give particular people and how you want them to benefit.

I. WHAT?

Personalty

Cash, receivables; rights under contracts; patents, copyrights, trademarks; stocks, bonds, other securities; mortgages, real and chattel; estates or trust-remainders or property subject to appointment; joint property interests; interests in pension or profit-sharing trusts; business interests.

Notes: ....
....
....

Real Estate

Residence; vacant land; improved property; leases; special tenancies; rights, such as easements.

Notes: ....
....
....

Life Insurance and Annuities

Proceeds; refunds and remainders; cash values; certificates of deposit.

Notes: ....
....
....

Miscellaneous

Interests subject to tax but not controlled disposition; personal effects; autos and other tangible personal property.

Notes: ....
....
....

II. HOW?

Outright Gifts

Of cash, property, securities, business interests, mortgages, personal effects, etc.

Notes: ....
....
....

Deferred Benefit Gifts

Such as vested remainders in trusts or following donor's retained life estate.

Notes: ....
....
....

Gifts of Income Only

Through living trusts, annuities, employment, whether for life or a period specified or contingent.

Notes: ....
....
....

Gifts of Dispositive Power

Such as special or general powers of appointment over trust funds, insurance or annuity remainders.

Notes: ....
....
....

Gifts of Benefit Rather Than Property

Such as third party beneficiary contracts in business transactions or the rendering of personal services for the benefit of another.

Notes: ....
....
....

PART III

TRANSFERS OF PROPERTY

CHAPTER XI

COSTS OF TRANSFER

Property may not be transferred without cost in one form or another. The usual transfers at death involve probate and administration costs, attorney's and executor's fees, state inheritance or estate taxes and federal estate taxes. Of all these items, the one of most concern to the estate planner is the federal estate tax. By far the largest slice of the estate will go for it. Because the tax must be paid within nine months from the date of death—if interest accruals upon its amount are to be avoided —the effect is often estate depletion far greater than the amount of tax involved. Excessive valuation of certain assets for tax purposes, the consequent increase in tax liability, and the necessity for sale and conversion of assets into cash for the payment of the taxes often result in a very high degree of shrinkage.

Federal estate taxes are progressive and are levied on a bracket system. Rates increase as the taxable estate grows larger, so that an estate owner who attempts to accumulate sufficient funds—in addition to what he already has—in order to pass his estate at par after taxes, is indulging in a highly refined version of a dog chasing his own tail. The tax fund will itself beget taxes at increased rates. For example, an estate of $350,000 must be increased about 32% to pass at par.

It is apparent that, after a certain point, it's no longer economical to continue estate accumulations in the usual manner. Some other means must be found to pass a reasonable proportion of accumulated wealth to heirs.

Speaking broadly, four basic approaches are available and may be used singly or in combination. They are:

(1) Continue adding to one's own accumulations in the hope that the after-tax net addition will build up to the desired amount.

(2) Give away part of one's existing accumulations, when it

seems that the point at which gifts can be made most economically has been reached.

(3) Use current surplus earnings to build separately-owned estates for other members of the family.

(4) Provide a tax exempt estate tax fund to make good the expected estate and transfer tax depletion.

The first method—that of continuing to add wealth to one's own estate in the hope that the rate of gross accumulation will be so great that the net after-estate tax increases will reach the desired levels—is illustrated above. Neither the second method— gifts of already accumulated property—or the third—the creation of separate property accumulations for beneficiaries rather than for oneself—is necessarily free of transfer costs. Both methods do substitute gift tax liability for estate tax liability so that the true tax cost is reduced because of the substitution of lower effective rates.

But an added true cost, discussed in Chapter VIII, is involved and must be considered: Both the income and personal economic benefits that would ordinarily be derived from the property given away are lost. The fourth method is essentially to accept the estate tax upon present accumulations and to offset it by providing a tax exempt fund outside of the estate and sufficient in amount to restore the estate and transfer tax depletion. Such a fund is most efficiently established by means of an adequate amount of insurance owned by heirs on the life of the estate owner. It does not matter whether the insurance is bought by the heirs out of independent funds or is given to them by the estate owner, who continues to pay premiums as gifts to the owners of the policies.

In the first instance, no transfer taxes are involved because the insurance proceeds are not part of the estate, nor are the insurance premiums transferred by gift. In the second, the premiums are gifts from the estate owner to the owners of the insurance policies and, as such, may or may not be subject to gift tax, depending upon the amounts involved and, perhaps, the extent to which the estate owner has previously used up his lifetime gift tax credit. Either way, the insurance proceeds comprising the fund will be beyond the reach of the estate tax levied at the death of the insured estate owner, so long as he has no incidents of ownership in the policies at the time of his death.

A reversionary interest is an incident of ownership, if it has a value greater than 5% of the value of the insurance proceeds, immediately preceding the death of the insured. But a reversionary interest is a right to have something returned to one and, as such, is a retained interest. It cannot exist in property that never belonged to one because such cannot come back. It exists only as to property that has been given away and that will find its way back eventually, if certain contingencies occur. That means that there can be no reversionary interest in property that has been given away and that comes back to the donor only through the action of the new owner.

The possibility that property that has been given away will come back to one is a reversionary interest and is an incident of ownership. It is this sort of thing:

John Jones gives an insurance policy on his life to his son, Jonathan, and provides that upon Jonathan's death before his own, the policy will go to Jonathan's son, Jason; but that if both Jonathan and Jason die before he does, the policy will come back to John. If John dies before Jonathan and Jason do, his estate includes a reversionary interest in the insurance policy. The possibility that John would outlive the other two and get the policy back has value and is a property right. It is valued as of the moment immediately before John's death, and without regard to his death, so the value is the actuarial computation of the probability that John will survive Jonathan and Jason. If that value is more than 5% of the value of the insurance policy, the proceeds will be included in John's estate and so will be subject to estate tax upon his death. But if John gives the policy to Jonathan and to Jonathan's heirs and assigns, he will retain no reversionary interest. Then, the mere fact that Jonathan might leave it to John or die without a will and leave John as his only heir does not constitute a reversionary interest and none of the policy values will be included in John's estate. Under those conditions, the only way that he can get the policy is through

Jonathan's act, whether that be the making of a bequest in his will or the failure to make a will at all—with the resultant inheritance by John by operation of law because he happened to be the next of kin.

The whole matter of property transfers involves the careful navigation of a narrow channel between the Scylla of estate taxes and the Charybdis of gift taxes. An understanding of the two levies, of the interplay between them, and of the way they work is essential; so some discussion is probably in point here.

Federal Estate Taxes

The federal estate tax is an excise tax levied on the transfer of property. It is neither a tax on the property itself nor on the right of an heir to inherit; it taxes the right of a deceased person to transmit property to persons of his own selection. It is imposed upon the net value of the estate at death and every transfer which is deemed to be in lieu of a testamentary disposition is subject to it.

Since the estate tax is levied on the right to transmit property, it permits the deduction of debts or obligations of the estate, administration and probate costs, attorneys' and executors' fees and other charges, but not the estate taxes themselves, from the total or gross estate as of the estate valuation date. [5] The result is the adjusted gross estate, 50% of which, but at least $250,000, is the marital deduction allowed for property passing to a surviving spouse in such a manner as to be includable in her estate upon her subsequent death. The adjusted gross estate then is further reduced by the allowable marital deduction, and the value of charitable bequests and what is left is the taxable estate upon which the tax is based.

Here is a chart showing how the estate tax base is determined:

(1) The value of all property owned by a decedent, plus the value of the decedent's interest in other property plus adjusted gifts = GROSS ESTATE.

---

[5] *IRC* 1954 §§2043(*b*), 2053-4.

Examples: Solely owned realty, personalty, insurance, personal effects; joint property; community property; certain powers of appointment; the then value of property given away within three years of death, and the gift taxes paid upon it; the gift tax value of other property given during life; the then value of property transferred subject to revocation, change, reservation of income and of transfers conditioned upon survivorship.

(2) GROSS ESTATE reduced by the allowable deductions = TAXABLE ESTATE.

Examples: Administrative expense, court costs, fiduciary and legal fees, debts and claims, funeral expense, marital deduction, charitable bequests.

NOTE: GROSS ESTATE reduced by IRC §§2053-4 deductions only = ADJUSTED GROSS ESTATE—50% of which is the topmost limit of the marital deduction in adjusted gross estates of $500,000 or more.

(3) TAXABLE ESTATE is the basis for computation of the ESTATE TAX.

(4) The ESTATE TAX reduced by credits for death taxes paid to the states, federal gift taxes paid on property included in gross estate, for federal estate tax paid on prior transfers, and the unified credit for estate tax = ESTATE TAX PAYABLE.

Certain types of property are taxed even though they do not pass by will. Thus life insurance, although it passes by contract and not by testamentary disposition, must be included in gross estate if the insured possessed any of the incidents of ownership at the time of his death, or to the extent that it is receivable by or for the benefit of the estate. The value of the right to appoint a successor to the benefits of a trust established by someone else may well be included in the gross estate, even though the deceased could never have taken full possession of the principal. Similarly, gifts made during life—but within three years of death —do not avoid the estate tax. Their value is included in the estate

and a credit for the gift tax is allowed against the estate tax
assessed. The subject has been discussed more fully in Chapter
IX, above.

Property to a certain value may be transmitted free of tax,
however. Under the Federal estate tax law the unified credit
allows the first $175,625 of property—of whatever kind—to be
transmitted exempt from tax, and the marital deduction removes
from gross estate, and so from the tax base, property passing
outright to a surviving spouse and not exceeding in value the
greater of $250,000 or 50% of the adjusted gross estate. Then,
too, any property which has been inherited or received as a gift
and tax-paid within ten years of the date of the death of the heir,
is at least partially exempt from the imposition of a second
transfer tax. The exemption is for full value if the heir dies within
two years; after that it decreases in amount by 20% each two
years to disappear entirely after ten years have elapsed. [6] The
estate tax law further provides for certain credits for state taxes
paid. Because state estate and inheritance taxes are always less
than the federal estate tax on the same taxable value and are
nearly always so adjusted as to consume the maximum credit
allowable against the federal estate tax, they are not taken into
separate consideration here. [7]

Here is an illustration of just how the federal estate tax is
computed:

Distribution: to spouse in marital deduction trust or outright, the
greater of $250,000 or 50% of adjusted gross estate; residue after
payment of all taxes, debts, other charges, to nonqualifying trust.

Gross Estate	$250,000	$400,000	$750,000
Deductions:			
Debts, claims, administration, etc.	12,500	20,000	37,500
Marital Deduction	232,500	250,000	375,000
Charitable Bequests	5,000	10,000	25,000
Subtotal	$250,000	$280,000	$437,500

[6]*IRC* 1954 §2013.

[7]*But state estate and inheritance taxes may alone apply to values too small to
attract federal estate tax—e.g., to gross estates of $120,000 to $350,000.*

Taxable Estate	-	120,000	312,500
Tentative Tax	-	29,800	91,880
Unified Credit:	-		
1977		30,000	30,000
1979		38,000	38,000
1981		47,000	47,000
Tax Payable	-		
1977		-	61,880
1979		-	53,880
1981		-	44,880

The table does *not* show that maximum use of the marital deduction in estates of less than $500,000—*i.e.,* those in which up to $250,000 may be taken if that be greater than 50% of adjusted gross estate—results in loss of the unified credit in the estate of the estate owner if he dies first, and shifts up to $47,000 more tax liability to the estate of the survivor. That is because each estate is allowed a uniform credit for estate tax, so that up to $175,625 (in 1981 and thereafter) can be passed free of tax by each spouse. Let's see what that means:

1. In the $250,000 estate, if we assume that $225,000 will be left at the survivor's death, the tax on her estate will be $62,000 subject only to $47,000 credit for a net tax cost of $15,000. In the $400,000 estate, $350,000 left at the death of the survivor will sustain tax of $104,800 before and $57,800 after the $47,000 credit.

2. Limiting the use of the marital deduction in the $250,000 estate—perhaps not very sensible in human terms—can eliminate all federal death tax on both deaths, since $125,000 marital bequest will be sheltered by the survivor's unified credit and the combination of the $125,000 marital deduction and the unified credit at the earlier death of the estate owner eliminates all federal tax there. Similarly, in the $400,000 estate, limiting the marital deduction to $200,000 will produce a tax at the survivor's death of $54,800 before and $7,800 after her unified credit while eliminating all tax at the earlier death of the estate owner since the marital bequest plus charity and other deductions reduce his tax base to $170,000 on which the $45,000 tax is offset by the $47,000 unified credit.

The estate subject to federal estate taxes contains many elements which are not ordinarily thought of as property, or as property being transferred by the decedent. The following checklist may be an aid in estimating the taxable estate:

1. Real estate, whether improved or unimproved

2. Personal property, including house furnishings, automobiles, jewelry, clothing, art objects and books

3. Stocks and bonds

4. Mortgages and chattel mortgages

5. Cash in bank and elsewhere

6. Accounts and notes receivable

7. Rights under contracts

8. Patent rights and other special property, such as copyrights, trademarks, etc.

9. Interests in business or professional ventures, including goodwill

10. Life insurance including: policies on his own life owned by the estate owner; policies on his own life owned by others, but in which he has any incident of ownership; policies on the life of someone else owned by the estate owner; policies payable to or for the benefit of the estate

11. Annuities providing either a death benefit, refund or survivor income

12. A power of appointment under a will or trust instrument exercisable by the estate owner through his will or otherwise, except for a so-called limited power and except for certain powers created prior to the passage of the Revenue Act of 1942

13. Property held jointly as a tenant in common or by the entirety to the extent to which it cannot be shown that someone other than the deceased contributed part or all of the purchase price [8]

---

[8] *An exception is "new" joint property of spouses under I.R.C. 2040(b) as amended by the Tax Reform Act of 1976.*

14. The principal value of any property which may
have been the subject of a gift—effective in poses-
sion or enjoyment only at or after death—and
subject to a reversionary interest greater than 5%
of the value of the property at the time of the
donor's death; the principal value of any property
given away subject to a retained right to enjoy
the income for the life of the donor; the value of
any property donated in contemplation of death;
and the value of the reversionary interest itself,
when property is given away subject to a reversionary interest that amounts to less than 5% of the
value of the property at the death of the donor.

Federal Gift Tax

The federal gift tax is complementary to the federal estate
tax. It applies to all taxable gifts made since June 6, 1932. Its
rates are progressive, just like those of the federal estate tax or
the federal income tax, in that the rate of tax increases as the
value of. gifts rises. The taxes apply cumulatively, so that the
tax base is never the amount of gifts made in any one year but
rather the total gifts made between June 6, 1932, and the end
of the calendar quarter to which the gift tax return applies. For
example, a man who has made $10,000 gifts annually for five
years is taxed in the fifth year, when he gives $10,000, on total
gifts of $50,000. The example presupposes that each year's gifts
were subject to tax.

The gift tax is imposed upon gratuitous transfers by a living
person, whether the gift be direct or in trust, and whatever the
nature of the property. For purposes of the tax, the word "gift"
has a meaning broader than customary and includes transfers
made for inadequate considerations in money or money's worth,
to the extent of the inadequacy.

But not all transfers are subject to gift tax. Gifts made before
June 6, 1932, when the gift tax was first enacted, are not. The
first $3,000 of gifts of present interest given to each of any
number of individuals in a calendar year is excluded from the
gift tax base. The first $100,000 of the value of outright gifts to

one's spouse, and 50% of the value of such gifts in excess of $200,000 is treated as a marital deduction and so is not subject to gift tax. (The *second* $100,000 gets no marital deduction, thus at and after the $200,000 level of gifts an ongoing 50% marital deduction is reached.) Gifts to charitable, educational, or philanthropic organizations; to the United States or a political subdivision of the United States; and gifts under which the donor reserves the right to divest the donee, or to revoke, are not subject to gift tax. [9] The tax on taxable gifts, like the estate tax, is subject to the $47,000 unified credit for gifts made in 1981 and thereafter. The credit "phases in" from $6,000 (1/1/77 to 7/1/77); $30,000 (6/30/77 to 1/1/78); $34,000 (calendar 1978); $38,000 (calendar 1979); and $42,500 (calendar 1980).

The gift tax is an excise tax imposed on the right to transfer property by gift during life. It is not a direct tax on property, but has the same nature as the estate tax. It applies to the fair market value of the property given, not to its cost as such, and is payable on or before the fifteenth of February following the year in which the gift was made, except that a return must be filed by the fifteenth day of the second month following the close of the calendar quarter in which all of the taxable gifts made during the calendar year for which a return has not been filed exceed $25,000. The $3,000 exclusion previously referred to was probably enacted largely for administrative convenience. It is applicable only to gifts of present interest, that is those which give the donee the immediate right to possession or enjoyment of the property. An outright gift is one of present interest, even though it takes the form of an insurance policy or a bond under which increased values may be enjoyed by refraining from immediate consumption of the values currently available.

---

[9]*Spouses joining in gifts to others may "double up" on both the credit and exclusions. They may give up to $6,000 in present interests each year to each donee and may take credit for $94,000 jointly. But each spouse's half of the joint gift is treated "as if" made separately, so that the credit allowed each of them separately does not spill over. For example, a husband who has used his total credit cannot use $15,000 of his wife's when a joint gift results in $30,000 tax. Only $15,000 would be allowed as she is deemed to be giving only half of the gift.*

Here are charts showing how the gift tax base is determined and an illustration of the computation of the tax itself:

(1) The value of all money or property transferred without consideration between December 31, 1976, and the end of the calendar year or quarter covered by the gift tax return, plus the excess value of money or property transferred within the same period, but outside the ordinary course of business, for inadequate consideration in money or money's worth = GROSS GIFTS.

> *Examples:* Outright gifts; gifts in trust; transfers that are sales in part, such as annuities bought from charitable organizations; etc., etc.

(2) GROSS GIFTS less: (a) annual exclusions, and (b) deductions allowable against current year gifts, plus: (a) aggregate taxable gifts made in prior years = TAXABLE GIFTS.

> *Examples:* $3,000 exclusion per donee for gifts of present interest; charitable gifts; etc., etc.

(3) TAXABLE GIFTS is the tax base. The tax computed upon it reduced by the tax computed at current rates on aggregate prior gifts = TENTATIVE GIFT TAX.

> *Assumptions*—Gifts made in 1977: $25,000 ABC stock to wife; $10,000 cash to son; $2,500 to friend; $5,000 cash to Harvard University.
>
> Gifts made in prior years: 1960—$30,000; 1972—$5,000; 1975—$10,000; total—$15,000 after taking $30,000 exemption in 1960.

Total Gifts, 1977		$42,500
Portion of gifts to son, friend, Harvard, reported by spouse*		0
TOTAL GIFTS FOR YEAR		$42,500
Less exclusions not exceeding $3,000 per donee (gifts of present interest)		11,500**
TOTAL INCLUDED AMOUNT OF GIFTS FOR YEAR		32,000
Deductions—		
Charitable (Harvard University gift less exclusion)	$ 2,000	
Marital (based on gift to wife)	12,500	
Specific exemption claimed	-	
TOTAL DEDUCTIONS		14,500
AMOUNT OF TAXABLE GIFTS FOR YEAR		$17,500
Total taxable gifts in prior years		15,000
TOTAL TAXABLE GIFTS		$32,500
Tax on $26,500 at current rates	$ 5,230	
Less tax on $15,000 at current rates	2,800	
TENTATIVE TAX ON TAXABLE GIFTS FOR 1977		$ 2,430
TAX PAYABLE		0

Note: A spouse making no gifts may consent to joint reporting on donor's return, so "double up" on the annual exclusions and on the unified credit. This was not necessary in our example. Moreover, in this case the consenting spouse would have had to file a return because her $5,000 share of the gift to the son would exceed her $3,000 exclusion for that donee. Her return would show total gifts of $8,750, exclusions of $6,750, and taxable gifts of $2,000, the $360 tax on which would use a comparable amount of her unified credit to net out at zero.

The gift tax and the estate tax are but two stages of a unified transfer tax which cannot be avoided by the simple expedient of making a gift rather than a transfer by will. The same tax rate applies to both kinds of transfers, as does the progression of rates. At death the taxable value of lifetime gifts made after

---
*See page 80.
**Three at $3,000; one at $2,500.

December 31, 1976 (and *more* than three years before the date of death) is added to the values to be transferred at death and to the date of death values of—and all gift taxes actually paid upon—gifts made within the three years ending on the date of death. The result is to apply the progression of rates to the totality of transfers in order to determine a tentative total transfer tax which is then reduced by the gift taxes actually paid on the gifts made in order to produce the net tax amount against which the unified credit is taken to determine the estate tax actually payable.

It's interesting to note that the unified credit applies against the gift tax, too; but only the gift tax paid in excess of the credit is counted as a prepayment of the unified transfer tax and the entire unified credit is thus moved forward to post-mortem application in full against the estate tax which is the ultimate transfer tax. (As we mentioned earlier in this book, the unified credit "phases in" from $30,000 in 1977 to $47,000 in 1981, and thereafter, affects the tentative tax on from $120,000 to $175,625 of taxable values.)

"Successful" gifts succeed in saving transfer tax only by eliminating from the gross estate of the donor these three items: first, any growth in the value of the gift property; second, the aggregate of the $3,000 per donee annual exclusions from taxable gifts allowed in respect to the gifts made; and third, any gift tax paid. But gifts may fail in these respects either because the donor's death occurred within three years of the date of gift —a circumstance that requires the date of death value of the gift and the gift tax paid upon it to be treated as transfers at death, so to be included in the donor's gross estate—or because the donor had retained the kind of string of control, discussed in a prior chapter, which makes the gift insufficiently complete to avoid reinclusion in the donor's estate at death.

Many of the things that the term "gift" includes, for tax purposes, might not be so thought of by a layman. Here is the list:

1. Outright transfers of property other than for an adequate consideration in money or money's worth

2. Transfers through joint tenancy

3. Withdrawals from joint bank accounts by the person not depositing funds

4. Irrevocable designations of beneficiary in those cases in which such a designation deprives the insured of the right to exercise any of the incidents of ownership without the joinder of the beneficiary

5. Contracts which may confer an immediately vested future benefit in someone else

6. Trusts which may confer an immediately vested future benefit in someone else

7. Forgiveness of a loan or debt

8. Sale outside the course of business for an inadequate monetary consideration, to the extent of the inadequacy

9. The irrevocable designation of a survivor-annuitant, as in the purchase of a joint-and-survivor annuity

10. The relinquishment of the right to revoke a previously established revocable trust, or of the right to exercise a power of appointment in favor of someone else

11. The commission of any act other than death which results in the final and complete transfer (other than for an adequate monetary consideration) of economic benefit and enjoyment in property to someone else.

The federal gift tax prevents complete avoidance of the transfer duties that would be levied at death if no gifts were made. Without it, property given away during life—in such fashion as to avoid inclusion in gross estate—would not be subject to any transfer tax. But it also offers considerable inducement to making lifetime transfers, because of the ability to move enhancement in value out of the donor's estate and to save transfer tax on the gift tax itself. These potential tax savings become even more attractive when the gift or series of gifts succeeds in moving highly taxed income from the donor's highest income tax bracket into lower brackets of the donees.

CHAPTER XII

BASIC TAX SAVINGS

Many things can result in tax savings. Some are simple, common-sense measures, such as: filing joint income tax returns to take advantage of the savings involved in splitting income, when one spouse has all or most of the family income; making joint gifts to obtain double exclusions and exemptions when one spouse's wealth is the source of the gifts; exercising simple care to take all proper exemptions and deductions. Some are complex measures, such as: the careful timing of capital gains and losses; the judicious use of installment sales, deferred compensation arrangements, private annuities; careful planning to make utmost use of the advantages found in differing state laws.

All kinds of taxes are involved, because an act designed to save estate tax so often alters the impact of gift and income taxes as well. Indeed, it should be considered in the light of all three and judged on the basis of total impact. But minimizing taxes is too broad a subject to deal with in full here, so we shall confine ourselves primarily to estate tax savings and touch upon the other tax effects only insofar as they follow from that.

Planning to save taxes by avoiding unnecessary tax liability is as legitimate an endeavor as any other form of economic planning. Adopting a tax saving mechanism that is recognized by the courts and the Treasury Department, that has been approved by competent authority and used in good faith, is the taxpayer's right and is neither illegal nor unethical. But resort to subterfuge, concealment of fact, or fraud concealed by technically correct form in order to present an operation in such a manner as to make it seem what it really is not, constitutes tax evasion. Such action is unethical and illegal.

Taxes must be paid in cash or in its equivalent in the form of certain government bonds. They must be paid within a definitely prescribed time to avoid the addition of interest, penalties or both. Hence, it is obvious that a corollary saving is made by maintaining sufficient liquidity so that tax obligations can be met when they become due, without the sacrifice of assets under unfavorable market conditions. That is a cardinal principle of tax planning. It cannot be too heavily stressed.

The simplest way to reduce or to avoid estate tax liability is to limit the assets of an estate to the amount of estate tax absorbed by the unified credit for estate tax. That amount we will speak of as the estate tax "exemption"[10] —but we will mean the taxable value generating only so much estate tax as is completely offset by the unified credit against estate tax: $120,000 in 1977, grading up in about $13,000 increments each year to $175,625 in 1981 and thereafter. What isn't there can't be taxed; hence, whatever can be got rid of in accordance with the rules, and actually is got rid of, must and will produce a saving in estate taxes. That is fundamental. There are several ways of applying the principle. All of them are basically simple, yet all of them may develop into, and be used in, highly intricate combinations.

Property in excess of the estate tax exemption may be held until death, transferred by will, and be exempt from estate tax, if the recipients of it are charitable, educational or philanthropic organizations, or the United States or any other of its political subdivisions, so long as it is not intended for use in a manner calculated to undermine, change, or influence government or legislation. This has tremendous possibilities in the larger estate.

Valuable and highly nonliquid art objects, books, scientific collections may be given away during life or willed at death to museums, libraries, universities, or to the public. Because of their great value, such assets add immeasurably to the estate tax liability, if something of this sort is not done; and the great difficulty of marketing them quickly for anything like their

---

10*An estate of up to $425,000 (after 1980) may pass totally transfer tax free between spouses, as the marital deduction is the greater of $250,000 or one-half the adjusted gross estate and the $47,000 unified credit offsets the tax on $175,000. If the $425,000 is left in trust so that $250,000 qualifies as marital property and the rest is used to give the surviving spouse a life income only, the children will inherit the $175,000 tax free because it was taxable on the first death and up to $175,000 more out of the marital property because of the unified credit available to the surviving spouse. At most, the $75,000 subject to tax on the second death will bear a transfer tax of $16,900.*

taxable value places upon the liquid portion of the estate an enormous drain for the payment of the taxes directly predicated upon these frozen assets. It is for that reason that Mr. J. Pierpont Morgan turned his very valuable library over to the people of the City of New York and engaged upon a long and carefully planned piece-by-piece sale of his art collection during the latter years of his life. It is the reason that Mr. Andrew Mellon— subsequently joined by several other public spirited and wealthy citizens—established, endowed, stocked with its first collection, and gave to the people, the National Art Gallery in Washington, D. C.

Although tax saving may not have been the principal motive, an estate tax of zero resulted when Supreme Court Justice Oliver Wendell Holmes left one-half of his estate to certain select charities and the other half to the Treasurer of the United States for whatever public purposes or application of general revenues he may desire to use it.

The same principle applies, but with less spectacular tax savings, when property of this nature is given away during life to the members of one's family, or to the friends who would ordinarily inherit it. The problem involved in such gifts is that the gift tax will have to be discharged out of other funds, since the property being given is a frozen asset that must be liquidated in its entirety or not at all. A measure of economy is achieved anyway, however, because the gift tax paid will not itself be subject to estate tax, nor will any appreciation in value of the gifts be taxed at death. Consequently, the estate tax will apply to a smaller taxable base and, since it is a progressive tax, may well be imposed at a lower rate.

The story is a little different when income producing assets are involved. Then the making of a gift is not only a matter of giving up something that adds to the joy, rather than to the tangible means, of living. It becomes a matter of giving away something in order to conserve property for others at a cost of presently enjoyable income for the balance of the estate owner's life. Much more sacrifice seems to be involved. But is it? Granted that the gift must be irrevocable, absolute, and immediately effective—it still need not result in complete economic deprivation. Often the contrary effect is produced when gifts of income-producing property are made to members of a close-knit family group, because not only are estate tax savings accomplished, but the family income is redistributed among a greater number of recipient taxpayers so that it is taxed in lower surtax brackets and the total family income remaining after taxes is increased.

> *Example:* A $2,000 yearly allowance is tax-free to the dependent, costly to the estate owner. Here's a comparison of the income cost of the yearly gift with that of a gift of property yielding $2,225 annually—a net of $2,000 to a donee paying the $225 income tax under the 1977 Table for single persons.

Giver's Tax Bracket	Income to Yield $2,000 After Taxes	Income Lost on Gift	Saving to Giver
25%	$2,667	$1,706	$ 961
30%	2,858	1,593	1,265
35%	3,078	1,479	1,599
40%	3,334	1,365	1,969
50%	4,000	1,138	2,862
70%	6,667	683	5,982

One way to achieve some redistribution of assets among the members of an intimate family group is to determine approximately how much a child, or other beneficiary, would actually obtain net of estate taxes out of the amount to be willed to him; then make a present gift to him of that net amount. The balance or estate tax portion of the contemplated bequest is used to pay the gift tax, if any, and to purchase a life annuity for the donor. As a result, the heir receives the full amount he would have netted after estate taxes, but gets it much sooner; the taxes on the balance of the estate are reduced because of the reduction in net taxable estate equal to the total amount actually given away, plus that paid in gift taxes and that used to purchase the life annuity; and, most often, the estate owner's income is barely affected or actually increased, because annuity income is largely tax-free and his entire income falls into considerably lower surtax brackets than formerly.

> *Example*: Annuity income is only partially taxable. Here is how an annuity yielding 5.7% on cost compares with fully taxable income when the annuitant's expectancy on the annuity starting date is 18.2 years (the factor for a male age 60 according to the table in the income tax regulations):

Income Tax Bracket	Taxable Equivalent of 5.7% Annuity
35%	8.66%
40%	9.35%
50%	11.19%
70%	18.52%
91%	61.26%

The formula for computing annuity yield in terms of fully taxable yield is:

$$T = A + \frac{100\,R}{(100-R)\,Ex.}$$

T is fully taxable yield; R is the applicable income tax rate; A is the annuity income as a percent of cost; and Ex is the expectancy of the annuitant on the annuity starting date and on the basis specified by government.

What's more, if the heir-donee sees fit sometime in the future to purchase insurance on the life of the estate owner—in an amount equal to the difference between the gift actually received and the amount that would have been willed to him—he will eventually get the full amount of his contemplated bequest without any reduction by estate taxes.

Another fundamental way to reduce estate taxes is to save the tax on the second transfer—that is, on the transfer from the original estate owner's heir to the heir's heir. This may be accomplished in many ways but they all involve the same basic principle —that of holding the capital fund in suspense for the benefit of the second succeeding generation and providing only income benefits for the first. Some examples are the use of a testamentary trust under which a widow is given lifetime income benefits but the principal is held for children;[11] or the designation of certain income rights under life insurance policies with the stipulation that payment of principal or of unpaid income balances is to be made to others at the death of the income beneficiary. Such a plan may even be accomplished without the sacrifice of necessary safeguards for the income beneficiary: power to invade the principal of the trust could be given to trustees when, in their own unfettered discretion, they determine that the circumstances of the income beneficiary require it.

A word of caution is indicated here in connection with powers of appointment. A fairly common practice is to give the income beneficiary—of either a trust or an insurance installment settlement—the power to designate, by will or otherwise, who shall receive the principal after the death of the income beneficiary. Despite the barrier erected between the income beneficiary and his actual enjoyment of the principal sum, it is included in the estate of the income beneficiary for estate tax purposes on the ground that the right to control disposition of the principal at death is merely a substitute for testamentary disposition and therefore a transfer within the purview of the estate tax.[12] Powers of appointment, if they are to avoid the imposition of an estate tax upon the death of the income beneficiary, must be so-called "limited powers" under which the income beneficiary may not appoint himself, his estate, his creditors or the creditors of his estate; but he may have the right to invade principal (i.e., appoint to himself) to an amount not exceeding $5,000 or 5% of the principal, whichever is higher, each year.[13] Under such limited powers, only the amount of principal that could have been withdrawn, but was not, in the year of the holder's death is includable in his gross estate on account of the power of appointment.

---

[11] *Useful in conjunction with the nonmarital part of the husband's estate or when no marital deduction is to be taken.*

[12] *For that reason such a "general power" of appointment does not defeat the marital deduction and is often used when assured trust management of marital property is desired.*

[13] *Such "limited powers" defeat the marital deduction.*

It's important to note here that the Tax Reform Act of 1976 imposes a transfer tax upon certain skip-a-generation transfers. Those affected are the ones in which a transfer to members of *two* or more generations below that of the donor result from the termination of the interest of an intervening beneficiary belonging to a higher generation. Put in English, it goes like this: a father leaves property in trust—or in any equivalent manner, such as insurance settlement options—to provide income to his widow, then to their child, and then principal to the child's child. The result is a tax on the death of the child, because both child and grandchild are members of generations younger than that of the father. But there would be no taxable generation skipping if the property after the widow's death went directly to the grandchild or was held to provide him with a life income. The next transfer tax, then, would lie upon the death of the grandchild. The reason? Only the grandchild belongs to a generation younger than that of the father-transferor so the "two or more generations younger" test has not been met.

There is also a fairly large group of what we will call precautionary tax saving methods. It consists of things to watch so that unnecessary estate tax liability does not result from careless, thoughtless, or just plain stupid management. For instance:

1. Certain government bonds are acceptable at par by the Internal Revenue Service in payment of estate taxes. It is just common sense to determine whether some of these bonds are in the estate; whether it is wiser to sell and utilize the cash for payment of estate taxes or to turn the bonds over to the Internal Revenue Service and be credited with their par value plus accrued interest. Strange as it may seem, executors have done the wrong thing in this regard, because only a few issues may be so handled, and even those need not be turned in but may be sold on the open market, if a more advantageous price can be obtained in that way.

2. Each state of the Union is looking for all the revenue it can get. Each state will tax at death any real property within its borders, and any personal property over which it can claim jurisdiction. Therefore, it is wise to make certain that corporate

stocks and bonds—issued by a corporation domiciled in another state—are fully protected by state reciprocity, else they will be subject to tax in more than one state at death. Similarly, it is plain common sense to establish definitely, clearly, and in as formal a manner as may be required, the actual domicile of the estate owner in one, and only one, state of the Union.

3. Business interests, rights under contracts, rights in special forms of property, such as patents or copyrights, are subject to varying degrees and methods of valuation. The Internal Revenue Service and the various state tax departments will do their utmost to place the highest possible value upon these forms of property, and in a good many instances succeed in taxing them at a value far beyond any price ultimately realized by the executor in the open market. Yet the estate tax value can be established in a manner binding upon government, if the business interest or property right is subject to a properly drawn contract governing the terms under which it may be sold. Such a contract can even be funded to assure satisfactory performance. That way it can be made to produce the contemplated values for the heirs, as well as to limit them for tax purposes. Surely it is evident that any steps that can be taken to establish a definite realizable value for these forms of property—and that can and do make that value binding upon the taxing authorities—are essential to orderly estate planning.

4. The estate is valued for tax purposes at the option of the executor, who may choose between the date of death and a date six months later. Since estate taxes do not become due and payable until nine months after death, it seems almost ridiculous to point out the wisdom of selecting the date of lower valuation. Yet there have been many estates in which this simple precaution has been neglected.

This is not a tax manual. Certain basic principles have been pointed out in this chapter . . . some of them have been expanded somewhat . . . but the list is not exhaustive and the methods of producing tax savings have barely been tapped. The entire purpose of the chapter is to indicate that tax savings are possible; that they are not necessarily confined to the huge accumulations of wealth; and that, essentially and in principle, they are not so complex as to be understandable only by so-called experts or specialists. They can be understood by the average intelligent estate owner. It is the putting of them into practice that requires the services of the tax expert, the experienced attorney, and the efficient life underwriter.

Let us summarize briefly the fundamental things that must be done or remembered to achieve basic estate tax savings. They are: maintenance of sufficient liquidity to enable payment of taxes without sacrifice of assets and without additions of interest and penalties; care in the exercise of the small, routine precautions that prevent undue tax liability; timely giving, so as to take advantage of the annually recurring exclusions and to eliminate the potential increases in value and even potentially payable gift taxes from the estate tax base; consideration of the family as one economic unit and consequent distribution of income producing assets among its members, so as to achieve both estate and income tax savings; provision of tax-exempt tax funds whenever possible; selection of the more economical method of accomplishing a given objective and of the more economic forms and methods of holding property; constant intelligent awareness coupled with sound professional advice.

PART IV

LIFE INSURANCE

CHAPTER XIII

LIFE INSURANCE AS AN ECONOMIC INSTRUMENT

There is nothing magical or mysterious about a life insurance policy. It is simply the scientific, mathematical application of the law of averages to the individual. Through the voluntary cooperation of many individuals, life insurance enables each member of a group to do what no man can accomplish alone.

Life insurance has always been an important economic instrument for the investor. It is the only practical means of anticipating future earnings and assuring their payment to heirs; of guaranteeing payment of specified sums at an unspecified time in the future; of overcoming the hazards of mortality and converting them into investment assets.

Only through life insurance can assured provision be made for the prompt and cheap payment of the obligations and costs which accrue at death, no matter when death may occur. Only through annuities—which are the reverse of insurance—can the hazard of long life be turned into an asset, making it unnecessary to conserve capital as a source of income for so long as one lives. Only the annuity principle allows scientific distribution of both capital and income over the term of life. These are the essential characteristics of insurance and annuities; the reasons for their continuing value as investments.

During the past thirty years or so, marked changes have taken place in our economic situation. Interest rates plunged downward, stabilized at very modest levels for a long stretch, returned to more effective yields about 1959, rose sharply in the late 60's and are now back to the more moderate 5-7.5% levels. Taxes of all kinds, and particularly personal income taxes, have risen to all time heights. The cost of living has inched steadily upward. The result is a marked increase in the relative value of insurance and annuities in the investment portfolio. Formerly insurance and annuities were used to underwrite certain contingencies, to hedge

against foreseen but unavoidable casualty, and thus to comple-
ment a carefully planned investment program. Now they may
be the essential element of the investment program.

The very nature of the insurance or annuity contract makes it
possible to accumulate substantial funds over a long period of
time in a tax shelter, because interest increments are not currently
available and so are not currently taxed. Any form of investment
that does not offer tax-deferred growth makes it necessary to re-
invest the income produced by capital and to compound it over a
period of years. That way income taxes come out of the income
first and only the after-tax amount is available for reinvestment.
The effective accumulative value of interest earnings is completely
lost on that portion of the reinvested income taken away in income taxes. In the insurance investment that problem does not
arise because accumulation is an inherent part of the contract
itself.

The tax preference shown insurance and annuity contracts
makes it possible to defer income tax liability even beyond the
maturity date of the investment proper, thus minimizing the
total tax liability on investment gains.

That is because the maturity values can be taken in the form
of income over a period of years or annuitized over a lifetime.
When that is done, the Internal Revenue Code pro-rates the cost
or "investment in the contract" over the selected income period
and only receipts in excess of that pro-rated amount are taxed.
The effect is to take the increment in value under the contract,
spread it out over the income receiving period, and tax it only
as it is received. When the decision has been to take income over
a specified term of years, the amount receivable tax-free each
year may be determined by dividing the cost or investment in the
contract by the number of years; the amount taxable each year,
then, being the excess of one year's receipts over the exempt
amount.

The same principle is followed when the maturity values of the
contract are applied to the provision of an annuity, but then
life expectancy, rather than a specified term of years, determines
the recovery of cost element in each year's income. Because of

the necessity of making special adjustments when two or more lives are involved, or when the annuity guarantees either a minimum number of payments or the return of a minimum sum of money in the event of early death, as well as the payment of a guaranteed amount for however long the annuitant may live, the computations can get pretty complicated. Usually the figures are provided by the insurance company whose contract it is . . . and it is just about impossible to determine ahead of time precisely what they will be in any given case. Just by way of illustration, the exclusion ratio, which is that percentage of the total income exempt from tax, seems to range from 63.5% to 97.6% for a male aged 65 and from 56.7% to 87.9% for a female aged 65, depending upon the type of contract involved and the amount of premium paid for it.

Present-day conditions inevitably drive home this cardinal principle of investment: It is wasteful to invest funds to produce current income beyond current needs because little of that income remains for personal use, after the payment of income taxes. Two corollary investment principles grow out of this one fundamental concept: Income must be so distributed that it will come to the individual members of the family group in such a manner as to subject it to the lowest possible income taxes; and wise, careful planning now is indicated if an estate is not to be dissipated needlessly.

CHAPTER XIV

LIFE INSURANCE AS A TAX SAVING INVESTMENT

Life insurance and annuities enjoy certain definite preferences under our present system of taxation. Life insurance paid by reason of the death of the insured is free of income tax in the hands of the beneficiary, whether paid in a single sum or otherwise.

Not only is the increase in value—represented by the difference between the face amount of the insurance and the cash value just before death—free of income tax to the beneficiary, but the means is at hand to provide her with a lifetime income that is substantially tax-exempt. Proceeds are included in the estate of the insured for estate tax purposes when they are payable to or for the benefit of the estate; when the insured is possessed of any of the incidents of ownership at death; or possibly when the insurance forms part of a trust established by the insured and subject to such retained controls as to bring the trust property into his gross estate. Annuities are treated favorably and granted partial tax exemption by the Internal Revenue Code which taxes only that part of the annuity income in excess of the investment in the contract, divided by the life expectancy of the annuitant.[14] The balance is tax-exempt for all time.

Several tax-saving applications of life insurance and annuities lie in the two rules cited above. On the basis of present-day income tax rates, the provision of tax-exempt income for beneficiaries means at the very least an increase of 14-20% in purchasing power. This—combined with the scientific distribution of principle as well as interest over the selected income period—makes for a tremendous enhancement in the income available to a beneficiary and makes it much easier to plan for the continuance of a reasonable scale of living. To carry this reasoning one step further, let us assume a potential beneficiary who has ample independent

---

[14] *"Investment in the contract" is cost of the annuity as of the income-starting date, less: (1) any amounts received tax-exempt before that time, and (2) an interest factor based on the value of any refund feature included in the contract. {IRC 1954 §72(c).}*

means. Then, the purchase of insurance on the life of an estate owner by that beneficiary (whether out of the beneficiary's own funds or through the medium of gifts from the estate owner) and the election to receive payment of the proceeds over a period of years or a lifetime under the Optional Modes of Settlement, would have two far-reaching and substantial results: (1) the insurance proceeds would be received at the death of the insured entirely free of estate tax; (2) the income payable from the date of death of the insured would be largely tax-exempt in the hands of the beneficiary, since the statute permits tax-exempt receipt of a pro rata portion of the amount that would have been paid at death in a single sum, and grants an additional $1,000 exemption for interest upon that single sum without time limitation when the beneficiary is a surviving spouse.[15]

Annuities are extremely effective when used as a means of distributing income amongst the members of a family group, because the income from the annuity will be receivable by the person to whom it is given so long as he lives, and is largely tax-exempt. If the family members are not old enough for the purchase of annuities on their lives to be practical, then it might be possible to predicate the annuity on the life of the person who is making the gift. Investment of the annuity income—or part of it—in insurance on the life of the annuitant, or in comparatively short-term endowment insurance on the life of the recipient, would enable replacement of the annuity income after the death of the annuitant. In any form, this use of annuities accomplishes three basic purposes: (1) it reduces the taxable estate of the donor; (2) it serves to increase the income of the family unit because annuity income is ordinarily far in excess of ordinary interest income, and the total family income will be distributed amongst several taxpayers; and (3) various members of the family are provided with independent funds which may be used, at some subsequent time, for their own investment purposes.

An even more effective way of distributing income among members of the family is the use of combination single-premium life insurance and annuity policies. Under this method, the sum

---

[15] *IRC* 1954 §101(d).

invested is divided between a single-premium life insurance policy (in a face amount equal to the total investment) and a single-premium annuity purchased for the difference between the amount invested and the cost of the life insurance. Ordinarily this combination guarantees approximately 2-1/2% to 3% on the total amount invested for the lifetime of the insured annuitant, then pays the principal amount of insurance at death.

Both contracts may be given to some member of the family group—or the annuity may be retained and the insurance policy given away. Such a transaction reduces the estate of the insured annuitant by the amount invested in the combination, whether both contracts are given away or the annuity itself is retained. That is because the insurance, not being owned by the insured at the time of his death, would not be includable in his gross estate (unless the gift of the policy had been made in contemplation of death) and the annuity would either have been given away or would expire at the death of the annuitant—either circumstance being sufficient to prevent its inclusion in gross estate.

When both contracts are given away, income is effectively distributed among members of the family group and net after-tax income of the family as a whole is usually substantially increased. Two factors account for that: (1) the income is distributed among a greater number of taxpayers and so is apt to be taxed in lower brackets than would have applied in the hands of the estate owner; (2) the annuity portion of the investment represents partially tax-exempt income and the insurance portion of it represents a tax-sheltered build-up of values in the form of increasing cash values during the lifetime of the insured—as well as in the form of the spread between the original premium paid for the insurance policy and its death proceeds.

Of course, a husband and wife, brother and sister, or any such combination could use this investment with perfect propriety and interesting results. For instance, each of them could purchase an annuity on his own life and each could then purchase the proper amount of insurance upon the life of the other. The result would be the provision of an adequate tax-free or largely tax-free income while both persons lived—and the provision of what should be largely tax-exempt income upon the death of one of the insureds. Since the annuity ceases to exist at the moment of death, and the cash value of the insurance policy on the life of the other is necessarily considerably less than the total amount invested, the estate tax liability of each of the parties to such an arrangement would be substantially reduced.

Annuities are also highly useful as part of an estate tax-saving plan. For example, gifts of income-producing property can be made during life, thus removing that property from the taxable estate at death, and the income loss suffered by the donor offset by the investment of another portion of his estate in annuities.

A fair measure of the gift in cases of this sort is the net amount the donee would have inherited had the property been left to him at death, subject to estate tax. As an example, take the case of an estate owner who plans to will $100,000, subject to an effective estate tax of 32%, to a daughter. Instead, he could give that daughter the $68,000 of her net inheritance and use the remaining $32,000 to pay gift taxes and to purchase an annuity on his own life for his own benefit. If he chose not to split the gift with his wife and if he had not used his unified credit previously, the taxable gift would come to $97,000 after the $3,000 annual exclusion and the tentative gift tax of $22,460 would be completely offset by his unified credit against gift tax (indeed, even in 1977, $7,540 credit would be left for future gifts and in 1981 the unused credit would be $24,540). That leaves $32,000 to invest in an annuity. If the gift were split between the spouses, the taxable gift would be $94,000 and each spouse would apply $11,060 of unified credit to offset it.

A sixty-year-old man could obtain a 6.61% return on a life annuity basis. After taxes that would provide a spendable income that compares very favorably with that obtainable on the $100,000 disposed of under the plan. [16] The result is to remove from his taxable estate at death the amount of the gift, that paid in gift tax and that invested in the annuity, as the latter ceases to exist upon his death. This sort of thing . . . done consistently over a reasonably long period of years . . . tied in with the donee's ownership of insurance upon the life of the donor . . . can go a long way towards maintaining estates intact for future generations.

---

[16] *See example on page* 89.

CHAPTER XV

INTEGRATION OF LIFE INSURANCE AND GENERAL PROPERTY

The integration of life insurance with the balance of an estate is a continuous process that begins with the purchase of the insurance and the purposes to which it is assigned. There are only two basic situations: insurance used to establish the capitalized value of a person's earning power and insurance used to guard against the depletion of other property.

Where there is no other estate but that represented by life insurance, we have the simpler of the basic situations. Here the entire estate and all of the benefits flowing from it must be provided by the insurance itself. The amount of insurance coverage should be based upon a fair capitalization of the earning power of the insured, thus establishing that basic capital in an entity entirely separate from the individual himself. One reasonable way to arrive at a man's capital value is to multiply his average annual earnings by his life expectancy and then to assume that approximately one-third of the result represents a return of capital and the remaining two-thirds pure earnings. While the formula is arbitrary, it is realistic in that it gives more weight to the human factor than to the capital factor and recognizes that man's productive period rarely exceeds thirty to thirty-five years. But this is just the beginning of integrated estate planning where insurance alone is involved.

In some cases the completion of inventions, books, plays, paintings, companies, or other projects of one kind or another might result in a substantial addition to the base capital value. These projects could, quite properly, be capitalized and hedged by insurance (probably term insurance because of its low premium outlay) in order to prevent loss to the estate of an asset that might well have been considerable but for the intervention of death.

In addition to these fundamental principles of capitalization, some attention must be paid to the income needs of the insured's dependents. To the extent that the capitalizations already indicated fail to provide adequately for dependents, additional income should be purchased through insurance. This part of the estate building process is less the process of capital conservation than that of income deferral to some future time and for the satisfaction of some future need. It is quite closely allied to investment in annuities for the estate builder himself, and it seems to make sense to use the higher premium and higher value forms of insurance for this portion of the program, in order to enable the achievement of the income needs of both the insured and his dependents through one plan.

The problem of capitalizing the human life value still exists, even in substantial estates composed of property other than insurance. But additional and more varied problems also exist in connection with the conservation of the other assets. If the estate funds are invested in property of a more or less nonliquid nature —and that takes into account almost all property other than cash, prime listed stocks, certain select bonds—one of the major problems is to provide liquid funds for the payment of estate costs, death duties and the various debts that must be paid at death.

Provision of these funds through insurance is both cheap and wise as it makes it unnecessary to hold money in highly liquid low yield investments, to sacrifice assets at forced sale, or to borrow. Even when circumstances dictate the purchase and the retention of the insurance by the insured himself, so that the insurance is subject to estate taxes, it will relieve the pressure on the balance of the estate. Any other assets subject to tax would probably return to the estate less than the sums invested in them; but it is the rare exception when life insurance remaining after payment of estate taxes will not show a net gain over the amount invested in premiums. (See table next page.)

When ownership of the insurance can be placed in persons other than the insured, whether they make the purchase out of their separate funds or the insured makes a gift of the premiums to them, this consideration does not arise Then the insurance proceeds are received entirely free of taxes and may be utilized to the fullest extent to loan money to the estate or to purchase assets from it. This caution is indicated, however: Insurance payable to an estate or for the benefit of an estate—regardless of

EFFECTS OF CAPITAL TRANSFER
Estate Owner Age 45

A. Capital transfer to single premium Ordinary Life:

A	B	C	D	E NET TO HEIRS	
				1.	2.
Net Estate	Amount Transferred	Face Amount Insurance	Tax Rate On Amt. Trans.	No Trans.	On Insurance
$ 100,000	$ 16,034	$ 25,000	28%	$11,544	$ 18,000
250,000	40,086	62,500	32%	27,258	42,500
500,000	80,171	125,000	34%	52,912	82,500
750,000	120,257	187,500	37%	75,762	118,125
1,000,000	160,342	250,000	39%	97,808	152,500

Notes: E1 = B x (100 - D); E2 = C x (100 - D).

B. Capital transfer to annual premium Ordinary Life:

A	B	C	D	E NET TO HEIRS			
				First Year		Gain	
				1.	2.	3.	4.
Net Estate	Amount Transferred	Amount Insurance	Tax Rate on Trans.	No Trans.	Insurance	10 Yrs.	20 Yrs.
$ 100,000	$ 988	$ 25,000	28%	$ 711	$ 18,000	$10,890	$ 3,780
250,000	2,471	62,500	32%	1,680	42,500	25,700	8,900
500,000	4,941	125,000	34%	3,261	82,500	49,890	17,280
750,000	7,412	187,500	37%	4,670	118,125	71,425	24,725
1,000,000	9,882	250,000	39%	6,028	152,500	92,220	31,940

Notes: E1 = B x (100 - D); E2 = C x (100 - D); E3 = C x (100 - D) - 10 E1; E4 = C x (100 - D) - 20 E1. Dividends will, of course, affect the result. If accumulated or used to purchase paid-up insurance additions, they will increase the benefit to heirs. If taken in cash, they provide tax-exempt income for the estate owner.

the source of the premium payments and regardless of where title may be—is taxable in that estate. Therefore, insurance owned by heirs in order to provide the liquid funds necessary for the purposes mentioned above must be used for those purposes only in the owner's own unfettered discretion.

When part of the assets of an estate owner consists of an interest in a business, insurance is the most efficient way to implement the sale of the business interest to surviving co-owners, or to a group of interested employees. It replaces a speculative and difficult asset in the estate with substantial liquid capital or with income benefits stemming from the insurance contract itself. As we pointed out in an earlier chapter,[17] this procedure involves a corollary estate-tax saving in that it requires a formal agreement pegging the value of the business interest and is binding upon government for estate tax evaluation purposes, thus preventing inflated appraisal of the asset and making it possible to plan for the payment of an accurately estimated tax liability.

Where the assets of an estate do not lend themselves to easy division except after liquidation, and where such liquidation would be inconvenient or would result in loss, insurance may be profitably used to equalize distribution to beneficiaries. Perhaps the commonest example of this situation is that in which an estate owner finds himself with some two-thirds or three-quarters of his net worth invested in a sole proprietorship and desires to provide adequately for a widow and a daughter, while giving his son control of the business. To allow his widow and daughter to share only in the remainder of the estate may not be enough for their needs. Then only two alternatives are open.

He can let the two women share in the business or its income, thus charging his son with responsibility for their welfare and putting them at the mercy of the hazards of the enterprise and dependent upon the son's sole judgment. Or, he may use insurance to equalize the discrepancy between the value of the business and that portion of the estate subject to division between the widow and daughter, in that way assuring

---

[17] *Chapter XII, page 91.*

them of the guaranteed, tax-exempt income that most perfectly fills their needs and prevents enforced interdependence of three members of one family group *who may also be members of antagonistic, or at least incompatible, economic units.*

Another interesting use of insurance may be made in connection with the marital deduction. If it seems desirable to leave existing property to others, or to a wife on such terms that the marital deduction would not be available, insurance can be used to double the estate—or to offset the value of the nonmarital property—without increasing the estate tax at all.

Note the estate tax effect of doubling an estate under $500,000 and how an estate of $500,000 or more may be doubled without increase in federal estate tax:

Adjusted Gross Estate	Marital Deduction	Federal Estate Tax * With M. D.	Without M. D.
$ 200,000	$200,000	$ 0	$ 54,000
300,000	250,000	10,600	87,800
400,000	250,000	38,800	121,800
500,000	250,000	70,800	155,800
600,000	300,000	87,800	192,800
800,000	400,000	121,800	267,800
1,000,000	500,000	155,800	345,800

In each case, offset by unified credit ($47,000 in 1981 and thereafter).

CHAPTER XVI

LIFE INSURANCE AND YOUR BUSINESS

Men go into business to provide assured income and capital values for themselves and their families. These objectives can be achieved only through management skill and experience. Management is human and subject to the hazards of mortality; yet it requires time to develop the techniques, skills and operating methods that build the business and make it pay. The very foundation upon which a high level of profit rests is the development of operating skills, methods, and techniques that produce efficient turnover of capital.

Sound management uses various forms of property insurance to protect the physical plant and tangible property of the business fully. It would not dream of operating without adequate insurance against fire, loss of use, theft, casualty, public liability, workmen's compensation, and the indemnity and completion bonds appropriate to its business operation. Taken together, all these forms of insurance indemnify against the loss of perhaps 10-35% of profits—those that stem directly from the employment of tangible values. The remaining 65-90% of profits is attributable to management and its ability to employ the tangibles efficiently and productively. Yet few businesses have adequately insured the management that alone makes possible the consistent build-up of capital values and the year-in, year-out production of high income that are the main reasons for the existence and operation of a business.

Many applications of life insurance to business needs have been accepted sound business practice for years. In principle, management life insurance is used to accomplish one or more of these purposes: (1) provide the additional working capital required when experienced management is replaced—in whole or in part—by less experienced successor management; (2) retire debt and give the business a new start; (3) provide additional working funds to hedge the loss of profit, the possible capital losses, the less efficient use of capital, some or all of which must be expected when experienced management gives way to new;

(4) provide funds to find and attract qualified replacement management; (5) create and guarantee a market upon which the business interest may be sold for full value; and (6) provide sufficient liquidity to the estate of the business owner, through redemption of a portion of his interest by the business itself, to pay transfer costs and taxes and so enable retention of at least part of a very high-yield investment in the estate's portfolio.

Life insurance buys time. It substitutes additional working capital for the accumulated skills of proven management, and so offsets the lesser decisiveness . . . the greater time required to implement policy . . . that almost always characterize the early days of successor management. Additional working capital acts to compensate for the highly developed familiarity and skill which have been lost in the change-over and which the successor management must acquire anew, even as it manages.

Life insurance effectively creates the additional working funds needed to cover possible losses and the almost certainly reduced rate of capital turnover, because the death of the insured inflates the relatively small percentage of earnings represented by the premium into the very substantial tax-exempt death benefits recoverable by the firm. Yet management life insurance is no more costly than the casualty and inland marine coverages routinely used to protect tangible values. Pure death insurance —term insurance with little, usually no, cash values—calls for as little as 1.5% annually of the amount of indemnity specified. It is akin to the property insurance mentioned.

Permanent insurance, such as ordinary life—creating cash values and useful as prime collateral—is comparable to the combination of depreciation reserves and casualty insurance on property, and calls for a premium lower than the charges for these two items combined—as little as 3% annually at the lower ages. Yet these minute quantities of earnings put into premiums on management life insurance guarantee substantial added working capital and create a large enough fund to make possible the discovery and attraction of seasoned successor management. That takes substantial money because what is needed is experienced management probably employed elsewhere, and the offer of a new job— replete with attendant risks and divorced from the security of established tenure—must be very attractive indeed if it is to be effective.

Especially in times of high tax rates, many businesses operate under a relatively heavy debt load. That's because they can do better for their owners by using earnings to retire debt, than by using earnings to pay out highly taxed dividends that must be reinvested elsewhere. Skilled, experienced management can stand up under heavy debt, but it is prudent use of current earning power to buy life insurance to underwrite the capacity of such management to clear up its debt and so guarantee the capital enhancement that would result from its discharge. It makes no difference whether the debt runs to the owners of the business or to outsiders. If the creditors are the owners, insurance used to clear off the debt will give their families a liquid position that will enable the discharge of transfer costs and death duties upon the value of the business interest and perhaps leave some cash over for investment in non-equity assets to counter-balance the estate's equity position. If the debt runs to outsiders, insurance used to clear it off will strengthen the company and enhance the value of the stock in the estate.

The usual, rather than the exceptional, circumstance is for the major portion of a businessman's estate to be completely tied up in his business interest. Not only is the largest portion of his capital tied up in his business, but by far the largest proportion of his income flows from that business. The yield on his equity investment far exceeds anything that can be expected upon reinvestment of that capital value in less hazardous securities. That same high yield will undoubtedly cause the assignment of an extremely high taxable value to the business interest in the estate of the owner and will aggravate the need for liquids and cash to pay transfer costs and death duties without forced liquidation of the business, and consequent sacrifice of its high values.

When the business enterprise is a corporation, the corporation itself is the logical purchaser of the business interest. Under a stock redemption contract, the corporation may agree to purchase the entire holding of a shareholder . . . part for cash . . . and part for a preferred stock interest which gives the estate a continuing stake in the venture. That preferred stock interest may be calculated so that it is equivalent to the value of the intangibles or the unrealized potential capital build-up, thus enabling the family to risk nothing that has already been created, while keeping a high-yield equity asset in order to average up the income of the estate.[18]

The division of the business interest into its tangible and intangible values for purposes of this sort may be accomplished by the application of a formula, often used by the Internal Revenue Service, for valuing business interests upon death. Most frequently that formula assigns a return of 10% to tangible and 20% to intangible assets. It is applied by taking the average annual earnings for five or ten years—exclusive of abnormally good and bad years—and subtracting from it 10% on net worth or invested capital. The remainder is then capitalized at 20% or five years' purchase, simply by multiplying by five, and the result of that capitalization is added back to the net worth to find the total capital value. The application of such a formula can separate out the values to be paid for in preferred stock from those to be bought for cash. It effectively bails out the estate, so far as the actual already created capital values at risk in the business are concerned. The percentage yields in the formula, of course, tend to vary with the nature of the business and the industry in which it finds itself. More stable businesses may reasonably be assigned a return of 8% or 10% upon tangible assets and 20% upon intangibles; while an extremely hazardous business, or one involving tremendous capital investment and long delay before returns are realized upon the finished product, may adopt a 15% or 20% return on tangible assets, and a correspondingly lower capitalization factor—such as 25% or 50%—to the return on intangibles.

One common way of applying the formula is to use the industry rate of earning on invested capital, then to capitalize the return on intangibles at somewhere between 10% and 100%, depending upon the hazards involved in the operation.

---

[18] *This must be done carefully. If the redemption contract gives the estate the right to choose between cash and preferred stock, all should be well. If the payment must be made in preferred, that stock may be "§306 stock" and so not saleable without attracting ordinary income tax on the full sales price.*

A business has great value to its owners, not only because of its high yield and the opportunity for capital build-up, but because it offers a comfortable working climate and a position of relatively untrammeled authority. Its value on the open market is a far different thing. There it will command merely the capitalized value of the earning power that the potential buyer believes to be available. It follows that the conservation and realization of the ultimate value of the business interest requires creation of a ready guaranteed market for its sale. Insurance can be used to create the buying power needed to guarantee the market provided by co-owners, employees, the business enterprise itself or an auxiliary entity, such as a profit-sharing trust.

Premiums paid for insurance upon the lives of its employees and payable to the business itself are not deductible. They come out of surplus; but that disadvantage is balanced by two major advantages: (1) the insurance policy is itself an asset to be carried on the company's balance sheet and to be used as collateral for credit purposes to the extent of its cash value, and (2) the insurance proceeds received on the death of the insured are tax exempt—and so much greater than the premiums paid that it is far more advantageous to recover them free of tax than to be able to deduct the premium at the cost of taking the spread between aggregate premiums and full death proceeds into taxable income when the insurance matures at death. Premiums paid by stockholders, partners, or employees to acquire their associates' or employers' interests are not deductible expenses in computing their taxable incomes either; but these death benefits, too, are receivable tax free. But insurance purchased by employees, or by a profit-sharing trust, in order to fund a business purchase obligation is usually paid for with deductible dollars so far as the business itself is concerned. Employees may be given reasonable salary increases, themselves deductible expenses, in order to give them the purchasing power to pay premiums.

Such salary increases are taxable to the employees individually, but usually at effective rates so much lower than those that would have to be paid by the employer as to make such an arrangement relatively tax wise.

One way of achieving the best of all worlds for the owner of the business, his heirs and a group of employees aspiring to ownership could also provide sound continuing management. It takes the form of a modest group bonus arrangement that guarantees the owner the full value of the business while transferring to the purchasing employees only a control block of from 60% to 75%, yet enables them to buy at an out-of-pocket cost far less than *either* the price they actually pay or the liquidating values they can reach immediately after assuming control.

Let's assume your business is worth $370,000 book value, that you would not sell willingly for less than $750,000 based on reasonable capitalized earnings and that liquidating value in a crunch would be, perhaps, $250,000. A sale of a 70% stock interest, effective at your death or upon retirement or disability, for $750,000 would leave your estate with $225,000 worth of stock —a 30% interest in earnings and growth—but with no capital at risk. That sale can be financed by life insurance upon your life owned by your corporation but subject to an arrangement—called "split dollar"—with a trust established by the corporation to administer a bonus arrangement for a hand-picked group of employee-purchasers. It's done by having the trustee and the corporation contract to share the insurance proceeds and values —corporation retains all rights to cash and surrender values and to death benefits equal to those values, trust obtains the right to all death benefits in excess of cash values. The cost is also shared —corporation pays the entire premium, but charges a government determined term insurance value to the trust each year and treats the amount so charged as a bonus paid to the employee-beneficiaries. As a result, the corporation deducts the bonus amount each year and incurs no costs other than lost yield on the cash value amounts which remain its property. The death benefit payable to the trust is kept level at the full amount of $750,000 by use of some of the insurance dividend (or return of premium) to provide additional term insurance in the amount of the cash value each year. The employees must pay income tax on their bonus amounts each year, but that is their out-of-pocket cost of acquiring ownership of your business. And in most cases, assuming the buying employees are in about 30-40% income tax brackets, the taxes paid by the employees if you live your full life expectancy will not exceed one-fifth of the insurance proceeds used to pay for their stock. Compare that with the one-third to one-half liquidity value! The deal itself is made between you and the trustee on behalf of the employees. You can arrange to add employees to the group, substitute for one or more members, discharge and remove from the group. Separate arrangements among the employees to take care of such changes in the group can and should be part of the formal plan.

Such a plan is not a do-it-yourself project; but competent counsel should have no major problems working it out for you.

An employer's contributions to a qualified profit-sharing trust constitute tax deductions; and the trust, in turn, pays the premiums upon the insurance it owns out of either the contributions it receives from the employer or its own tax-exempt income from the investment of those contributions.

Even though corporate owned insurance must be paid for with nondeductible dollars, it offers a high return to the firm. The insurance proceeds are tax-exempt at the death of the insured, so that money comes in net and is worth more than twice as much as ordinary taxable business profits. For example, here are rough figures showing the investment value of a dollar of ordinary life insurance on a fifty-year-old executive:

| | If death occurs in: | | | |
	5 yrs.	10 yrs.	15 yrs.	20 yrs.
Corporate investment	$.20	$.40	$.60	$.79
Gain to corporation	.80	.60	.40	.21
Equivalent profit before tax at 50% rate	1.60	1.20	.80	.42
Equivalent annual taxable yield compounded (approximate)	—	30%	12%	4%

Both dividends and insurance premiums come out of profits after corporate taxes; but the double taxation of dividends at high rates often makes it sensible to use available profits to strengthen the corporation itself. Here's a comparison of the value of money kept within a corporation and used to maintain insurance on key men with the value of that same money paid out as dividends to stockholders: At the end of ten years, $3,235 a year used to pay premiums on ordinary life insurance on the life of a 45-year-old executive adds to the corporate pocketbook $20,800 in cash value, plus the potential of a tax-free gain at death running from $100,000 down to $80,000. Over a ten-year period, that same $3,235 a year distributed in dividends to a stockholder in a 50% tax bracket and able to invest at 4%

compound interest will add only $17,800 to personal capital. If the $3,235 annual payment is divided so that $1,450 is put into premiums on $100,000 term insurance protection and the remaining $1,785, which would go to build up cash values in the ordinary life policy, is distributed in dividends, the ten-year result is $9,900 more in the stockholder's personal estate compared to the $20,800 more in corporate assets resulting from the investment in ordinary life.

The opportunity for capital appreciation at capital gains rates is what makes most men go into business for themselves. They recognize the premium value of fattening up a business. A large earner in high income tax brackets can create more wealth for his family by building capital values in his business and passing them on free of income or capital gains tax than by taking dividends which must pass through the personal income tax sieve and attempting to reinvest what is left. Earnings can be built into capital value by plowing them back into new facilities, operations and earning power; by anticipating them and borrowing for expansion with the purpose of using both old and new earning power to retire the debt; or by using some earning power to maintain insurance on owner-executives or key men to underwrite earning power and debt retirement and bring in a tax-free return.

Conservative investment might produce 4% on capital. Then, in a company that can earn 20% a year on its invested capital before taxes, management produces the spread of 16% per year before, 7.68% after, taxes at a 52% corporate rate. Only 2% of the actual after-tax net used to maintain management life insurance can indemnify against the loss of the executives who produce the superior earning power. If the company is worth $250,000 and makes $50,000 before, $24,000 after, taxes; 20% of its net is $4,800 and buys $120,000 insurance at $40 per thousand premium. Upon the owner's death, the $5,000 used for premiums, and worth only $3,000 or less if paid out as dividends, guarantees his family an additional $120,000 to take up some of the slack between a 4% investment yield and a 20% management yield. Here are the mathematics (all figures rounded approximations):

Year	Paid-Up Insurance	Cash Value	Distribution as Dividend in 40% Personal Tax Bracket Compounded at 2%
2	$8,880	$5,779	$6,180
3	14,520	9,573	9,360
5	23,520	15,960	15,924
10	43,680	31,747	33,507
15	60,600	46,920	52,917

Corporate owned life insurance is valuable, too, when the company has opportunity to expand and earn its 20% before-tax profit on additional invested capital. If the company borrows $100,000 at 6%, it sets up $20,000 additional pre-tax earnings, must pay $6,000 interest and $7,280 taxes and retains $6,720 net. Little more than half of the additional after-tax net, or $4,000, put into $100,000 management life insurance lets the company: (1) keep its original $24,000 net after-tax earnings intact and more readily available for retention and compounding to clear off the debt; (2) get about $4,000 additional net after-tax income to compound and use for the same purpose; (3) have insurance to underwrite full debt retirement upon the death of management; (4) establish a $450,000 net worth—$100,000 of it in liquid insurance—upon retirement of the debt out of earnings while management lives ($250,000 original net worth, *plus* $100,000 borrowed and repaid out of earnings, *plus* $100,000 insurance proceeds on subsequent maturity of the policy by death); and (5) eliminate all personal income and capital gains taxes on the build-up.

PART V

FAMILY PLANNING

CHAPTER XVII

MARITAL DEDUCTION PLANNING

In some states—Arizona, California, Idaho, Louisiana, New Mexico, Nevada, Texas and Washington—the basic law is—or came through—the old Spanish or the French. Those "community property" states recognize the marital community between spouses and, as a result, all of the wealth that accrues to a husband and wife during marriage is owned by each of them in equal shares.

That is true of accumulated wealth and it is true of the earned income of each spouse, as well as of the income from the investments of the community. It is not necessarily true of property the spouses owned individually before marriage, or of property inherited by or donated to one of the spouses during marriage.

Such noncommunity property is called "separate property" and the income from it is separate property too. In the eight community property states, the death of one spouse works a transfer of only one-half of the community, and, of course, of any separate property owned by the deceased. It doesn't matter which spouse died or which spouse created the wealth. The husband who made the money still can control the flow of only half of it at his death, so only half of the community is treated as his for estate tax purposes. The principle works both ways of course. The wife who didn't make the money still can control one-half of the community, so one-half of it is taxed as part of her estate at her death, even though her husband survives her.

Most states are common law states whose concepts of property and ownership derive from the English common law. In those states, each spouse is considered to own the property that he or she created, inherited, or received by gift, with full control of that property during life and at death. Some exceptions for the protection of spouses are to be found in the law, but they do not go to the heart of ownership. In common law states, for instance, a husband cannot deprive his wife of a certain minimum interest in his property upon his death. Under the old common law this was the dower (wife's right) or curtesy (husband's right) to at least the income for life from one-third of the real estate. In our society, real estate—to most families—means a dwelling, not income-property like a farm, so most states have replaced or bolstered dower by a statutory right of election that enables a surviving spouse to claim against the will of the deceased.

The rules vary as among the states, but a common provision is that a survivor must be left at least one-third of the real estate—and in many states of the personal property as well—or she is entitled to take the equivalent in value "against his will", no matter what the provisions of the will may be. Frequently that one-third interest of the wife's is absolute and she is entitled to that much of the property, without any strings whatever attached. As a result, if a husband leaves his wife just the statutory value but puts it in trust in an effort to control its flow after her death, she may "take against the will" to the extent of breaking through the trust restraints and taking the property as her own absolutely. Unlike the principle of community property, however, the two spouses do not each have title to or own one-half of the wealth and the income created during marriage. Each owns only what he or she has earned, inherited, received by gift, or otherwise acquired, and the restraints against disinheriting a surviving spouse are restraints in law against being able to cut that spouse off without an adequate share in the property actually owned by the deceased. That means that if a husband has earned and created all of the wealth of a family in a common law state, he must take care of his widow up to certain specified minimum limits, or the law will allow her to take that much property regardless of his desire. However, it is *his* property and her death before his does not result in her being able to dispose of a single penny, because she has no rights of ownership.

Back in 1948, after many years of unequal income and estate tax treatment of the residents of community property states and common law states, the Congress enacted the marital deduction as part of the United States Internal Revenue Code.

The marital deduction attempted to equalize the tax treatment of families living in community property states and those living in common law states, by providing that the husband or wife who actually owned the property in a common law state could leave up to half of it to the surviving spouse and deduct the amount actually so left from the estate tax base of his estate. In that way the estate tax treatment of common law and community property families was equalized.

The same principle was applied to gifts between husband and wife and the spouses in common law states were permitted to deduct half the value of a gift from one spouse to the other, so that just the remaining half became the base for the application of gift tax, if any. Similarly, spouses in common law states were permitted to join in gifts to third persons and treat such joint gifts as though each spouse had actually given half, no matter who owned the gift property. That gave them equal gift tax treatment with spouses in community property states, since its effect was to double up on exemptions and exclusions and reduce the progression of tax rates. Finally, to equalize income tax treatment, the spouses were permitted to file joint income tax returns; to compute the tax upon one-half of the net taxable income shown on the return; and to pay double the tax so arrived at. Going through that rigamajig made it possible to avoid the progression of tax rates and held the tax paid upon an income of $20,000 to the smaller amount that would have been payable on two incomes of $10,000 each—exactly the situation in a community property state.

Actually the estate tax marital deduction is the most important tool available in planning the flow of property through the family; and the effective use of the marital deduction at death is the most important aspect of marital deduction economics in planning. Husband and wife can do little to affect their joint income tax liability by making gifts to one another during life—because the filing of joint income tax returns produces the same amount of tax as would result from actually dividing their total incomes equally between them. For that reason, dividing ownership of property between them does not accomplish anything. Indeed, following up such gifts by the use of the full marital deduction, upon the death of the first spouse to die, tends to defeat itself because it concentrates wealth in the estate of the surviving spouse and tends to generate a high estate tax there.

Next in importance is the right of spouses to join in gifts to others so that each is treated as making one-half of the gift, even though all of the property given away belongs to only one spouse. The effect of permitting such joint giving and joint tax treatment is to allow two unified gift tax credits instead of one, and two exclusions for gifts of present interest each year to each of any number of recipients. So it becomes possible for a husband and wife to give away up to $351,250 free of tax, in addition to *annual* gifts of $6,000 to each of any number of people. It doesn't matter how hedged around with restrictions as to time or use the gifts of $351,250 are; but the annual gifts of $6,000 per donee must be pretty much unfettered so that the property is immediately and completely available to the recipient, since the annual exclusion is allowed only against gifts of present interest and these are defined as gifts of property as to which the donee has "the immediate right to use, possession and enjoyment."

An important exception is that gifts in trust for minors are treated as present interests, against which the exclusion may be taken, if the trustee has sole discretion to use the property given and the income from it for the benefit of the minor up to his age twenty-one *and* that property, plus any accumulated income, must go to the minor at age twenty-one or to those he designates or his heirs at law if he dies during minority.[19] Note that the trustee need not *use* this power; but he must have it.

Probably the two most common types of wills are those in which a husband leaves everything he has to his wife without planning, forethought, or restriction—and those in which he hedges everything he has left her to such a degree that he must obviously have thought her a ninny. The first character gets a full marital deduction willy-nilly. Since he has left everything to his wife, he has certainly left the maximum value for which a marital deduction can be taken. He saves an estate tax at his death; but because he's left everything to his wife, he has simply deferred the problem, and gained some time for the payment of tax, at the

---

[19] *The federal statute* [IRC §2053(c)] *is written in terms of age 21, so new state laws reducing the age of majority to 18 or any other lesser age do not govern here.*

cost of paying more tax than is necessary. You see, half the estate will be taxed at his death and then all of it will be taxed at hers. The second character, who has been over-protective, will get no marital deduction at all because the kind of trust arrangements that he uses do permit his widow to dispose of anything that she has inherited. He's taken care of all of that. Nothing will be taxable in her estate and, for that reason, she hasn't received enough ownership in any of his property for his estate to get any marital deduction.

If we look at the problem purely from the standpoint of mathematics, the most efficient use of the marital deduction is for one spouse to leave the other just enough property in qualifying form so that the values subject to tax at the death of each spouse will be exactly equal. That saves money because the tax on each of two estates of equal size, whatever the size, is less than one-half the tax on a single estate equal to their aggregate value. Estate tax rates are progressive too. Dividing the estate so that part will be taxed at the husband's death and part at the wife's sets up two full unified estate tax credits and that helps save taxes.

From the mathematician's standpoint, the ideal procedure is to add the value of the husband's estate to the value of the wife's and divide by two. Each spouse leaves the other just enough to equalize the two estates. Obviously if the husband has all the property and the wife none, he would try to qualify half of his estate for the marital deduction. She would have no problem, since she has no property to leave in the first place unless she survives him when presumably she will have no husband to leave it to and to qualify it for the marital deduction. If the husband's estate is worth $200,000 and his wife's is worth $50,000, the mathematics indicate that the husband ought to leave the wife $75,000 of values qualifying for the marital deduction, because that would give us two estates of $125,000 each. The wife, obviously, would be better off to leave her husband whatever she wished in such form that it did not qualify for the marital deduction. The taxes on her property at her death will be lower than the taxes on any of her property added to her husband's estate and taxed at his death. Indeed, in this example, both spouses' unified credits would eliminate the taxes if the wife survived.

So far that's all very well, but how do we know what will qualify for the marital deduction and what won't? How can we consciously and deliberately go about getting the results we want?

Well, property qualifies for the marital deduction when it "passes" from one spouse to the other in such form that the survivor will be taxed at her death if the property is still in existence then. Property passes in that way when it is left to a surviving spouse outright or when she gets it by survivorship, inheritance or operation of law. So it qualifies for the marital deduction when a husband makes a will under which he gives it to his wife absolutely. It qualifies when a husband dies without a will, because then his wife takes her share by inheritance under state law and she gets complete ownership and complete right to dispose of the property in any way. Likewise, when a husband and wife own property in joint name or by the entireties so that the survivor takes all, the property qualifies for the marital deduction because there are no restraints on what the survivor may do with it. Operation of law is a little more complicated, but really all that it means is that property qualifies for the marital deduction when the wife elects to take her outright share against her husband's will or when it goes to her absolutely and without restriction because the law says it must—for example, as when a husband dies leaving a will that is not valid because not properly witnessed or that may not be admitted to probate.

All this does not mean that a husband cannot protect his wife against the loss of property or income or against the demands of children and other relatives by providing for professional management and administration. He can give her the advantages of skilled professional stewardship by using trust arrangements that conform to certain requirements of law and by using insurance income settlements that conform to certain other special requirements.

For instance, a husband can leave his "marital property" to his wife in trust and can limit her to the income from the trust. He can even name their children or anyone else he wishes to take an income interest or a remainder interest in the property after his wife's death. But to do that and get the marital deduction he must be careful that his wife has the right to all of the income from the trust at least annually and has the added right to name those people who will take either income or capital upon her death. This is the so-called "power of appointment trust" under which the surviving spouse has the right to appoint people of her choice to take the trust property no matter what her husband has said shall happen to it if she does not exercise her power to appoint. Her power to appoint must include the right to appoint to her own estate so that she can control the flow of the trust properties through her will and she must have the right to exercise her power "solely and in all events", without interference or restraint from anyone else. Substantially an identical requirement governs the qualification of insurance proceeds left to a surviving spouse under income options in the insurance policies themselves.

Interestingly, property left to a surviving spouse in trust may be left under such terms that she gets none of the income at all, so long as the trust terminates at her death and both the trust property and the accumulated income are paid over to her estate so that their disposition is governed by her will. This is a so-called "estate trust" and it qualifies for the marital deduction under the same provision of the law as does property that is left outright.

Certain kinds of property cannot qualify for the marital deduction no matter what we do about them. That is true of terminable interests under which someone else will get an interest in the property or the property itself after the interest of a surviving spouse has been satisfied, if that other person receives his interest in any manner except as the result of a purchase at full value. That concept is a little tough so perhaps an example would help:

A man owns rental property, such as an office building. He gives the property to his son but reserves the rental income for thirty years. He dies with twenty years' rents still to come and bequeaths the right to get them to his wife. His estate cannot get a marital deduction for the value of the right to rents bequeathed to his wife. That's because at the end of the original thirty-year period the son will step in and take over the property in which the surviving spouse had an income interest measured by the rentals. The son acquired his right to the underlying property by gift from his father, so the right to rental income inherited by his mother from her husband is the kind of terminable interest that does not qualify for the marital deduction. But if the father had sold the property to his son and reserved the same right to the rent for thirty years, he could bequeath his right to rental income to his wife and get a marital deduction for its value. Then the interest of the son in the property underlying his mother's income right would have been acquired by purchase and her interest is not the kind of terminable interest that is disqualified for the marital deduction.

Interestingly while a husband's estate will not get a marital deduction for the value of a life estate or an income estate for a term of years in property that goes to someone else after the life estate or income estate has been satisfied, it will get a marital deduction for the value of a remainder interest left to a surviving spouse, even though someone else's life estate or income estate for a period certain must be satisfied before she gets the property.

We said before that from the viewpoint of a mathematician the ideal way to use the marital deduction is to use just enough of it to make sure that the estates of husband and wife will be equal in size. That's true enough, but the mathematician's point of view is sometimes pretty unimaginative. Human problems enter into the decision as to the most efficient way to use the marital deduction.

For example, the marital property escapes tax at the husband's death and will be subject to tax at the wife's; but if she uses it up during her lifetime, it won't be in her estate to be taxed. Doesn't it follow that a husband whose estate is not too large might be very wise to use the largest possible marital deduction for a young wife who has great opportunity to consume all the marital property before her death? A good example is marital property in the form of life insurance that is paid out to the wife-beneficiary in the form of an annuity income for life. She will get maximum value out of that kind of marital property, because she will get the greatest possible spending power and the smallest possible residue subject to tax at her death, yet she cannot possibly outlive her income.

Contrast that with this situation: A surviving wife keeps the marital property intact for her children. Her only living benefit from the marital deduction is whatever income is produced by that part of her husband's estate that would have gone out in estate tax had he not used the marital deduction. If the marital property was worth $100,000 at the husband's death and the saving in estate tax because he used the marital deduction came to $20,000, the added annual income of the widow who kept her $100,000 of marital property intact would be limited by the yield on $20,000. Yet she could consume the $20,000 itself over her lifetime without reducing the children's inheritance one penny. That's an important consideration when estates are small enough so that pure income will not be sufficient to maintain the standard of comfort that the wife should have. It's also important when the estates are so large that whether the children get a few thousand dollars more or less is of no moment, because in that situation income taxes are so high that the surviving spouse's spending power can be maintained only by having recourse to principal in some scientific and regular manner. This concept is explored more fully in the next chapter.

CHAPTER XVIII

SOME MARITAL DEDUCTION MECHANICS

Whatever the relative value of the marital property to the total property of the husband, the most efficient way of utilizing the marital deduction seems to be through the use of two trusts: (1) a marital trust and (2) a nonmarital trust. The marital trust may be either the power of appointment type under which the wife gets all of the income and may substitute her own estate or other people of her choice for those her husband specified as successor-beneficiaries, or it may be of the estate type under which the entire trust property becomes part of her estate no matter whether the income was paid out to her during her lifetime or simply accumulated and added to the principal of the trust.

The nonmarital trust may provide anything that the husband-testator wishes, but it does not provide for the addition of the trust property to the wife's estate nor does it give her a taxable power to appoint successor-beneficiaries. The reason for the distinction is that no tax is paid upon the value of the marital trust when the husband dies. It is deferred until the wife's death. But the tax on the nonmarital trust is paid at the husband's death and no tax is to be paid subsequently upon the death of the wife or of any other income beneficiary of that trust.

The usual pattern is to set up the marital trust as a power of appointment trust and to give the widow all of the income from it, the right to name those to whom the trust property will go at her death, and sometimes the right to draw down principal at her discretion as well. Then she is also given the right to the income from the nonmarital trust and the trustees of that trust are given complete discretionary power to advance whatever principal they feel is needed to maintain the wife in proper circumstances. If the income from the two trusts is enough for her to live on, and if those two trusts each represent one-half of the husband's estate, that arrangement just about forces the property of the marital trust to be taxed at the wife's death because it will be in existence then.

There is a way of using the two-trust principle and still re-ducing, possibly even eliminating, the estate tax on the marital trust. That's done by providing that the wife shall receive all of the income of the power of appointment marital trust and so much of the principal of that same trust each year as is equal to the after-tax income of the nonmarital trust. Then the non-marital trust provides that the trustees shall accumulate the income, adding it to principal each year, until the marital trust has been exhausted, when they are to start paying out income and enough principal each year to maintain the required level of payments to the surviving wife. Let's take some figures and see how this would work:

Assume a $200,000 marital trust and a $200,000 non-marital trust each producing $8,000 a year and ignore the income taxes on nonmarital trust income, to keep the example simple. Under this variant the surviving widow would get $8,000 income from the marital trust and $8,000 principal of that trust the first year, and $8,000 income of the nonmarital trust would be added to principal. Each year the widow would get whatever the income of the marital trust happened to be plus so much of the principal of the marital trust as equals the income of the nonmarital trust for that year. As time went on, her income and principal payments combined from the marital trust would decrease gradually. Her spending power would not decrease in proportion to the decrease in the number of dollars of her income because the principal payment out of the trust would not be subject to income tax at all. It is net and so very much more valuable than an equivalent amount of income. At the rate of $8,000 a year it would take twenty-five years to ex-haust the principal of the marital trust. At the end of that time, if she were still living, and if the trustee had been able to accu-mulate the income of the nonmarital trust at even 3% after taxes, that accumulated income would have added $261,368 to the value of that trust and none of the added value would be subject to tax in the surviving wife's estate, while the entire $200,000 of marital property would have been consumed and so would no longer be in existence to be taxed at her death.

Of course, if it seemed desirable to put a minimum income floor under the wife, the instructions to the trustee could provide for earlier payouts of income in amounts needed to maintain the wife's total receipts from the two trusts at a minimum level, or for the payment of specific items, such as medical costs, when receipts from the marital trust fall below a set level.

Using the marital deduction merely creates time in which to plan. That is true whether it is used to equalize the estate or to throw the major burden of the combined tax (normally paid on the deaths of both husband and wife) onto the estate of the wife or second to die. Buying time, though, is one of the basic principles of estate planning and often makes it possible to avoid the sacrifice of very valuable assets. Since using the marital deduction is a way of buying time, use of the marital deduction can be combined with creation of an estate tax fund which will itself be tax-exempt at the death of the husband and at the death of the wife because it will not form part of either estate. Such a fund can be created by the use of a term trust by the husband. We'll discuss term trusts as well as other trust arrangements in detail in a later chapter, but this kind of trust runs for a short period of time during which the income is paid out or accumulated for later distribution to whomever the trust instrument names as income beneficiary and at the end of which the principal comes back to the person who created the trust.

Now a term trust is effective to shift both the trust income and the income tax upon it to either the trust or the trust bene- ficiary, depending upon whether income is accumulated or dis- tributed, and provided the trust property cannot come back to the grantor of the trust in less than ten years. The point here is: If a husband takes income-producing property and puts it in trust for his children for fifteen years, reserving the right to get that trust property back at the end of that time, he can provide that the trust income shall be accumulated by putting it into premiums on life insurance on his wife's life. Then, at the end of the trust term, any trust income that has been accumulated in other forms and the insurance policy on his wife's life . . . or its proceeds if she died sooner . . . are turned over to the children and the original trust property comes back to him. In many cases, trust income used to pay premiums will be taxed to the husband-grantor, but the rest of the income will be taxed to the trust and—if counsel drafts the trust skillfully—*none* of the trust income will be taxed to the husband even though paid in premiums. It will all be taxed either to the trust or to the children.

If the husband who created the trust would be taxed at 60% on the trust income and the trust and, perhaps, the children, are taxed at only 25%, 35 cents out of each dollar is effectively saved for family purposes. That 35 cents is diverted from the payment of income tax to the payment of premiums on life insurance on the wife's life and that insurance will come to the children in replacement of the taxes that were paid on their father's death, or as a fund with which to buy assets from their mother's estate, so that her executors will have the cash with which to pay taxes, or both.

As a matter of fact, the trust can provide that after fifteen years either the original trust property or a number of dollars equal to its value on the date the trust was executed shall be returned to the husband-grantor, but that the trust itself shall go on for the life of the beneficiary or for any other lawful period. Then the trustee will collect the insurance proceeds upon the wife's death and he will have the funds that can be used to loan money to her estate, or to buy assets from it—if that seems wise in his judgment. If it does not seem wise, he will at least have money that represents part or all of the estate tax depletion at the death of the husband and wife and will be able to invest that for income for their children.

Since there is no reason to use one trust when several can be used, it is often wise to establish such a trust in the form of a single entity for purposes of administration and management— but in the legal form of separate trusts for each of the child-beneficiaries. If that is done for, let's say, three children, it will provide three separate trust taxpayers and the aggregate income tax paid on the income of the three trusts will be taxed at the lowest possible level—somewhere around 20-22% on up to about $8,000 aggregate income—as opposed to the rate that would apply to the same number of dollars taxed on top of the father's income—in our example, 60% or better. Such a term trust recaptures a considerable number of dollars that would otherwise be lost in income tax and applies them to the implementation of the family plan. It creates funds that are exempt from estate tax at the death of the creator of the trust, at the death of his wife and, possibly, if the trust is so drawn, at the deaths of their children as well. So it may save up to three estate taxes. It may save some estate tax, too, if the grantor dies before getting back the trust property. The value of his right to get the property back is taxed in his estate, but it is a discounted value based on the number of years still to elapse before the reversion occurs. In the first year, when reversion is still 15 years off, it is 59.7% of the value of the property and increases gradually to full value.

The gift tax involved is pretty small. It is based merely on the value of the right to the income from the trust, since the principal is to come back to the donor. If the trust is for 15 years, for example, the value of the gift is the value of the property placed in trust minus the value of the right to get that property back at the end of 15 years. The net value for gift tax purposes in a case like that is 58.27% of the value of the property. That's not very expensive giving.

Such an arrangement can save capital gains taxes, too, in those cases in which the property put in trust is apt to increase in value materially during the trust term. The trick here is to limit the amount that returns to the grantor to the value of the property at the time it is given to the trust. That keeps capital enhancements in the trust and out of the grantor's estate. It makes realized capital gains taxable to the trust—possibly at a rate lower than the 25% rate limit applicable to the first $50,000 of capital gains in any year. That is because capital gains are not taxed unless the property is sold or exchanged or otherwise disposed of, and the maximum 25% rate doesn't apply until the taxpayer is in a 50% income tax bracket. Only then is 25% of the total gain equivalent to 50% of the one-half of the gain taken into account for income tax purposes.

Up to that point, tax can be paid at regular income tax rates at the taxpayer's option because he is entitled to select the cheapest way of returning the gain. That makes it possible for a trust whose income is taxed in minimum brackets to retain more capital gain net after tax than the creator of the trust who would be forced to pay at a 50% rate on that gain. In any event, the term trust can save estate taxes on the increase in the value of the trust property, if it provides that the grantor will not get back the trust property itself but the number of dollars equivalent to the value of the property on the day it was placed in trust. That keeps the value of his estate at the same level and keeps any increase in value of the property in the trust for the trust beneficiaries. There that increase in value will not be taxed until the trust property is taxed and that might not be for three generations.

But how do we solve the problem of giving back to the grantor only part of the value of trust property that has not been sold? If stocks or bonds are involved, the reversion is paid off in fewer shares or bonds and, when necessary, in fractional shares or bonds that have been divided into the proper size chunks. If real estate or other property that can't be cut up is involved, the whole shebang goes back to the grantor—but he gives the trust a mortgage for an amount equal to the excess value. In that case, mortgage interest appears to be deductible by him, and feeds the trust; amortization payments give the trust added cash principle to re-invest and diversify.

CHAPTER XIX

TRUSTS ARE USEFUL

The classic means of reducing tax on a family's income is to multiply taxpayers, so increasing the number of exemptions. That causes the income carved off the top of that of the head of the family to be taxed in the lowest brackets of the recipients. But, many years ago, the courts held that the fruit cannot be divorced from the tree and that the mere assignment of income—without an accompanying assignment of the underlying property—is ineffective to shift the income tax from the owner of the property to the one who actually gets the income itself.

Still, it is always possible, and often wise, to give income-producing property to other members of the intimate family group. Doing so can effectively conserve many dollars otherwise lost in frictional income tax waste and put them to work for family purposes. The effect of such an action can be dramatic. For example, $4,000 investment income that would yield only $1,880 net of tax to a man whose other taxable income comes to $60,000 can be diverted to a child who has no other taxable income and no deductions or exemptions to offset against it and increase the retention for family purposes to $3,452 each year. The $1,572 difference mounts handsomely over a ten-, fifteen- or twenty-year period even without interest, and the added results of earning 3% compound interest after tax upon it will not be unacceptable to your children.

Probably the most efficient way to divide income among the members of the family is to use trusts. They can be used for your wife, your children or anyone else you wish to benefit. To the extent that the trusts actually distribute the income or have it available for distribution, it is taxable to the beneficiaries. To the extent that the income is or must be accumulated by the trust, it is taxable to the trust. Any number of trusts can be used. You are not limited to one trust per child, for instance. You may have several trusts for each child; varying their terms just enough to justify the existence of multiple trusts. You may provide that some income is to be accumulated and some distributed and in that way have part taxed to the trust and part to the individual distributees. You may even leave the shares of the individual beneficiaries very fluid by using what is called a sprinkler device. That is simply an instruction to your trustee to accumulate or pay out the income each year as he sees fit, and to pay so much to each of the beneficiaries as he believes is required to meet certain objective standards you have put into the trust instruments. That makes it possible for the trustee to give your daughter more money in a year in which her children face very heavy medical expenses, for example, while giving less money to your sons who have enjoyed good business and have already high incomes; yet to change or even reverse the pattern the very next year if that seems indicated.

Not all gifts in trust effectively shift income taxes from the person who created the trust to others. For instance, you will be taxed with the income of the trust you create if the trust is revocable so that you can take back the trust property; if it is irrevocable but the trust property comes back to you after too short a duration; if you or the trustee or someone else whose interest is not substantial and clearly adverse to yours may cause the income to be distributed to or accumulated for you or your spouse; if the trust income is used to meet your legal obligations; if it may be used to pay premiums on insurance on your own life or that of your spouse, except for trust-owned insurance solely held for approved charitable purposes.

Income-Tax Savings

So if you want to save tax on the trust's income, you must really give the trust property away. There are no problems if you give it away utterly and forever. There are no problems, either, if you give it away for a specified term of years after which the original property or the equivalent dollar value is to come back to you. But if you do that, be sure that the gift is for at least ten years. A trust that is supposed to last the life of the beneficiary can actually return the property to you in less than ten years if that reversion occurs only because of the death of the beneficiary. The trust will still be effective to shift tax on its income, even though the beneficiary is so old that it would be highly unreasonable to expect him to live ten years or more.

You can retain important administrative powers, such as to vote the stock held by the trust, direct or veto trust investments, re-purchase trust assets—privileges that are very valuable if you are going to put stock of your own company into the trust and that is something you might well want to do. But such powers must be exercised in a fiduciary capacity or with the consent of some-one in such a capacity, so you'd better be trustee or—preferably—co-trustee with an "independent" person. A trust company is best because "related" or "subordinate" parties are presumed to be subservient so that their actions are attributable to you. Your spouse (unless legally separated), parents, issue, siblings, em-ployees, corporations in which your stockholdings and those of the trust are significant from the viewpoint of voting control, and em-ployees of such corporations are all "related" or "subordinate" parties unless their interests in the trust property are adverse to yours. You need the independent trustee or co-trustee particu-larly if you may need to borrow from the trust. Otherwise, such loans must be repaid in full with interest by the end of the taxable year, even though they call for adequate interest and are based upon adequate collateral.

You can use trusts for your children and still not give up the $750 dependency exemption you may have for each of them. While a child is under nineteen, it doesn't matter how much income he has so long as you contribute over half his support. If the trusts distribute $750 a year to a child over nineteen and not a student, his income will be below the level at which he ceases to be a dependent. If the trusts accumulate income for the children, the same result follows. When a child is ready for college, the trust can pay more than $750 to him and you will still keep your $750 exemption so long as you pay for more than half of his support. He will pay the income tax on the income distributed to him so long as none of the money is used to pay for his necessary support and education, which remain your legal obligations while he is a minor. If the trust income is used for that purpose, it may well be taxed to you. Even then, you're getting a bargain because the income tax on the child's expenses must be less than the expenses themselves. But if it is used for educa-tional travel in the summer, to buy a car, for extra books and things of that sort, it will be taxed to the child because such expenditures are not your legal obligations, even though they may be highly desirable and of great benefit to the child.

In Estate Planning

Trusts have many and varied uses in estate planning. You can create a trust for a fifteen-year period to accumulate income for a grandchild, so that he will be assured of the necessary money to complete his education. If you are to get the trust property back after fifteen years, the taxable value of your gift is only 58.27% of the value of the property; but the effect of the gift is to save and accumulate for the child the difference between the percentage rate of income tax you would have to pay on each dollar of trust income and the rate actually paid by the trust. That can mount pretty sharply in a fifteen-year period.

You can create a trust to maintain insurance on your life, your wife's life or your children's lives. Properly done, it will result in a good portion of the premiums being paid out of what would otherwise be income tax dollars.

You can use a trust to keep deductible business or professional expenditures within the family. That's done by creating a trust for, let's say, your children and selling your business property to the trust. The rent that you pay will come to more than the taxes, interest, and other deductible expenses you pay as owner. It probably will have to, since the trustee must get fair market rates for the property, including the use-value of the land. The great benefit is that you can deduct that rent from your top-bracket income and the trust can accumulate the amount in excess of necessary expenses in the lowest bracket for future family use.

You can use a trust to accumulate business profits that you do not need for current living expenses. Suppose that you now take $50,000 or more in combined salary and bonus and really have no need for more except for investment and accumulation for the future. Suppose you were to recapitalize your business and issue some Class B stock calling for dividends in a minimum amount before any payment may be made on other classes of stock and on which the dividend requirements would be great enough to use up the bulk of the declared dividend. That Class B stock could be put in trust for your children and the dividends accumulated for them. Once again, the judicious use of a sufficient number of trusts could cause that income to be taxed in the lowest possible tax brackets with a material over-all saving for the family.

You can use a trust for your charity, too—and save money in the process—if charity appeals to you so strongly that you feel a continuing moral obligation to give substantially year-in-year-out, whether business is good or bad. In a good year you can buy income-producing securities and put them in trust for charitable purposes. If you have more than one chance in twenty of getting the securities back, you can't take a current income tax deduction for the gift to charity. But if the trust is for fifteen years, say, and your wife or child is to get the securities at the end of that time, the gift to charity is at least 58.27% of the value of the securities—and probably more since the charity must receive either an annuity of a stated amount or at the least 5% of the value of the trust as of the end of the previous year if that proves to be greater than the actual income—and it is an income tax deduction so long as you don't exceed the maximum percentage of income allowed for such gifts.

The gift to your wife or child is only 41.73% of the value of the securities and can be offset by your unified credit and, in the case of your wife, is cut in two by your marital deduction as well. Each year you may distribute the income of that trust to such charities as you may desire, yet it will not be taxed to you.

If you are ambitious to give a new laboratory, a new dormitory, or some other outrageously expensive gift to a worthwhile charity, you may put income-producing property in trust and accumulate that income for distribution to the charity—or for use in the construction of the building for that charity—at the end of the term of years when the fund created by accumulating the income will have grown large enough. Once again, you get a deduction for the gift in trust and the trust income accumulates income tax free because a tax-exempt charity is to benefit by it.

Non-Tax Uses

But income tax savings are not the only reasons for using trusts in planning estates. Business continuity, the protection of children by a prior marriage, the maintenance of a residence for someone you love, the opportunity to preview your estate in operation, the opportunity to make substantial financial arrangements without publicity or embarrassment of any kind—these are all purposes that can be very efficiently served by the intelligent and skilled use of trusts.

Business continuity is often a matter of getting good interim management for a few years until your son grows up and can take over. That management can be of the sort supplied by a good corporate trustee—in that it can be limited to overseeing the operations of an active employed management—in much the same fashion that you would supervise if you were retired but still an interested and informed stockholder. More and more trust companies these days are willing to accept trusts that consist of minority stockholdings or limited partnership interests, with the understanding that a controlling interest will go into the trust under the businessman's will. More and more, these professional trustees are willing to enter into the councils of your business—while you are alive—by means of taking a seat on the Board of Directors . . . or of participating in the management council of a partnership or a proprietorship. In that way professional supervision for management can be brought into the business on a standby basis so that the whole process of becoming familiar with the operation of a particular business and of the personalities involved in running it may be accomplished before the actual job of full time supervision has to be undertaken.

That saves a great deal of breaking in, loss of profits and loss of decisiveness in action. It may be the one way to keep for the next generation that profitable family business and the unusually high income return it offers. Of course, properly done, such an arrangement can result in shifting both income and the tax on it to the trust; but then the trust must be one of those that does effectively shift income taxes—such as the irrevocable lifetime trust or the ten or fifteen-year or longer term reversionary trust we mentioned before—and the trustee must have true independent control of both his interest in the business and the business profits distrlbuted to him.

Trusts are very useful when dealing with rather delicate marital affairs. Sometimes wives or husbands die and the survivors remarry. Often, when that happens, the survivors have children by the earlier marriage and property that came to them from the previous spouse. It seems reasonable to safeguard that property for the children of that marriage. Yet the laws of most of our states give a spouse certain definite minimum rights in the property of the husband or wife and, in doing so, might well take a substantial portion of that property away from the children whose father or mother had originally owned it. Perhaps the only satisfactory way of discriminating against the new wife or husband and in favor of the children of the earlier marriage without going through the unromantic legal process of getting a waiver of interest from the new spouse is to establish trusts for those children before the second marriage takes place. Now, those trusts don't have to deprive the surviving parent of income from the property while he lives; they just have to deprive him of the right of passing that property on to anyone else. They are irrevocable trusts in favor of the children, but subject to a reservation of the income for the life of the parent. Made before marriage, they effectively block the claim of a spouse to any of the property.

Sometimes, too, as Dr. Kinsey points out, people have extra-marital arrangements and feel sufficient love and obligation to their extra-marital partners to want to provide for them; but do not wish to subject the relationship or the surviving party to the glare of publicity. Then a living trust made in favor of the person you want to benefit is the only answer (other than life insurance or an annuity contract). It is a private contract and its details cannot be uncovered and released to the public through the newspapers or otherwise by anyone who is merely probing. Such a trust need not be irrevocable and it need not be immediately effective. It is sufficient to use a revocable trust that permits you to change your mind at any time during life, because it becomes irrevocable upon your death and diverts the flow of income from the trust property to the object of your

bounty. The trust can be so set up as to give the income beneficiary the right to dispose of the trust principal if you wish . . . or
it can cause the trust principal to come back into your own estate . . . or to flow to your children after a term certain or after
the death of the beneficiary, whichever you happen to prefer.

Often a husband will use a residence trust to receive income
and to pay the expenses of a home for his widow. The usual
provisions are for the widow to have the right to occupy the home
without cost, and the courts have held such an arrangement not
to be taxable to her. Because one of the major purposes of a
residence trust is to conserve the property for children or others,
it is wisest to have the trust pay only the costs necessary to preserve the property for the estate, so its payments should be limited
to taxes, interest, amortization, insurance and maintenance. There
is no reason for limiting the proportion of those items paid by
the trust to the proportion of the residence occupied by the widow.
The trust may pick up the entire check; but it probably should
not go so far as to pay for living expenses, such as servants'
wages, heat, light, telephone bills and other things that do not
tend to preserve the property for the estate. Those items would
almost certainly be taxable income to the widow and might conceivably jeopardize her tax-free receipt of the other benefits.

Sometimes an estate involves substantial values that require
careful management and specialized skills, at least for a predictable period of time. Then, it might be very wise to use a
revocable trust instead of relying merely upon a will. The estate
assets can be put into such a revocable trust with the estate owner
as co-trustee. Since the terms of the trust can be changed, or the
entire arrangement adandoned, at will, the effect is to give the
estate owner an opportunity to preview his arrangements for
his family and to both observe and train his survivor-trustees in
the way to carry on after his death.

One of the by-products of the use of living trusts is the utter
privacy that attaches to the trust device. The provisions of a
trust are not a matter of public record but of private contract.
Persons who have no legitimate and provable interest are not
entitled to information; hence there can be no undesirable publicity at any time. Contrast this to the testamentary trust which

is part of a will and so a matter of public record and the advantages, in certain situations, become very evident.

Where True Accumulation Is Not Proper

A word or two must be said about the accumulation of trust income. Several of the states do not permit accumulations except during the minority of trust beneficiaries or for limited and specified periods. Many do permit accumulations within the limits of the rule against perpetuities; which means that a trust may accumulate income during the entire period of its legal existence.

When the trust is to be used as a shelter for the accumulation of income, then, you must be certain that such accumulations are proper in the state of your residence or you must go outside of that state to establish the trust under more favorable laws. That that can be done by choosing a trust company or other trustee resident in the more favorable state. Often it isn't necessary to go to that much trouble. Many states that do not permit accumulations beyond the minority of the trust beneficiary nevertheless permit the quasi-accumulation trust under which income accumulation does not occur because of a mandate placed upon the trustee but because of permissive discretion granted to him. Under the quasi-accumulation trust, the trustee distributes so much income as he in his sole discretion feels is required by the income beneficiary, and accumulates the balance for later distribution to that beneficiary.

Eventually, either upon the death of the beneficiary . . . at some prior time in the discretion of the trustee . . . or at the termination of the trust during the lifetime of the beneficiary, the accumulated income is distributed. Thus the essential difference between the accumulation trust and the quasi-accumulation trust is that the former may treat the accumulation of income as part of the trust principal; the latter treats it merely as a retention of income for subsequent distribution to the beneficiary and never adds it to the principal. For that reason, strong anti-accumulation states, in which accumulation is permitted only during minority—like New York before September, 1958, when the law was changed—have held that the quasi-accumulation trust is perfectly proper, since what takes place is not accumulation but merely a temporary withholding of income. Whether the technical, legal definition be withholding or accumulation, the federal income tax result is the same: income not distributed because not distributable is taxed to the trust.

CHAPTER XX

TRANSACTIONS WITH FAMILY MEMBERS

You can make business deals with members of your family and so get both income and substantial capital appreciation into their hands. If these deals are made on a fair basis so that the terms are such as would be produced by arm's length negotiation with independent strangers, they will stand up tax-wise. But because they are deals with members of the family, it is even more important than ordinarily to get the details down in writing, to formalize every transaction, to be certain that the facts show that the other members of the family, or the people acting for them, acted independently and in their own best interests.

Here are some of the things that can be done, some of the ways of getting more utility out of family income.

Loans

You can lend money to your children to go into business for themselves. Instead of charging interest, charge a stipulated percentage of the new business' profits. As long as the facts show a real debtor-creditor relationship, the borrower will get a deduction for the "rental" he pays for the money under a contract calling for repayment of the loan on demand, plus the payment of a specified percentage of profits while the loan is extant.

Leases

You can rent business property owned by other members of your family at the fair market rental for that kind of property. Sometimes the lease calls for a flat dollar amount, sometimes it calls for a percentage of earnings. One method is to make a gift of either property or cash to an irrevocable trust. Then the trustee can lease back the property at a fair rental, or can use the cash to buy property from your business and lease it back at a fair rental. The trust must be irrevocable; the trustee must be independent; and the rent must be fair. A corporate trustee is preferable. This arrangement has been tried scores of times and the courts have gone along with it and permitted the rental deduction when an independent trustee represented the family members to whom the property was given. But the courts have often treated the arrangements as a pure tax dodge when there was no trustee and the property was merely given to a spouse or a child over whom the donor presumably could exert influence.

For transactions of this sort to work, tax-wise, you must be able to show that you gave up control and economic benefit, as well as just title to the property. That's why an independent trustee is so important. He's charged with the duty of looking out for the best interests of the beneficiaries of the trust, even though that might hurt the interests of the donor of the property. His duty requires him to make the best deal and exact proper security. It's worth it, though, in many cases. For instance, a doctor owned a clinic building on which he was deducting taxes and $650 depreciation each year. He gave the $40,000 building to a trust for his wife. The trustee leased the building to him for $6,000 a year. That gave him an enormous saving in terms of income taxes recaptured for members of the family and reduced his taxable estate as well. Another couple transferred coal lands to trusts for their children and leased the land back on a royalty basis. They actually operated the mines and paid the trust up to $20,000 yearly in royalties—and the Court of Appeals found that the royalties were deductible by them and taxable to the trusts. In both these cases, there was a large spread between the 20-30% tax rate payable by the trusts on the rental income and the 50% or greater tax rate that would have had to be paid by the parents.

Joint Ventures

On occasion an opportunity to invest some money and make a considerable gain occurs. Then you can use a joint venture with members of your family, so that shares of the gain will be taxed to them and will never become part of your estate to be taxed on your death. A joint venture is a kind of partnership for a definite period—usually short—and for a definite deal or purpose. The contracts that set up the joint venture control the accounting, management, duration, expense handling and methods of dividing profit and loss. The joint venture being what it is, you don't even have to give any part of the initial capital to the family members you take in as joint venturers. You can put up the capital and specify in the joint venture contract that that initial capital is to be repaid before any sharing of gain, although you may specify, if you wish, that the other venturers must bear their shares of loss. But there are advantages, even if you make an actual gift of part of the initial capital to the other venturers, because the amount of your gift for tax purposes is fixed at the value of the capital interests you give away. That much is out of your estate and represents some estate tax-saving to start with. Then the profits of the joint venture are divided from the very beginning and are taxable to the venturers in proportion to their interests. They never form part of your estate so never add to your estate tax base. Instead, they form part of the separate estates of the other members of the family who have been taken into the venture with you.

You can lend your children your business skill and ability and let it build separate estates for them. This can be done by giving them a little money or a little property and then managing it for them so that the income and the increase in value flow to them. To be successful, you'd better have separate books for them and identify the property and the funds pretty clearly— no commingling with your own funds and no indiscriminate use of your credit for their benefit.

One example of how to do this properly involves a cow, a calf, an eight-year-old boy, a smart father and $17.24. The father gave his boy the $17.24 by opening a bank account for him and, a couple of years later, gave him a cow and a calf. Seven years after the opening of the bank account the balance on hand was $760 and the cow and calf had multiplied to sixty head of cattle. In addition, the then fifteen-year-old boy had over 600 acres of land worth $10 an acre, a leasehold covering another 60 acres and a $6,000 annual income.

The courts held that the income was taxable to the boy not to the father because: (1) separate books were kept for the boy's business; (2) his cattle were branded with his separate brand; (3) his funds were kept separate and not commingled with his father's; (4) bank loans made for the boy were secured by his property, though endorsed by his father; and (5) money drawn from the boy's bank account was used only for his business expenses. His support and maintenance were paid for by his father. The results of the arrangement were the creation of separate capital for the boy—and the accumulation and reinvestment of income taxed to the boy—at rates considerably lower than would have been applied if that same income had belonged and been taxed to the father.

Real Estate Sales

Suppose you own rental real estate worth considerably more than you paid for it. If that's the case, you'll probably find that the depreciation deduction you get now is pretty low in comparison with the one that you could get if you had bought the property at today's prices—and that difference in depreciation deductions is equal to a difference in taxable income. This is just another way of saying that more of the rent you receive is subject to income tax than may be entirely necessary. Now, if you sell that property to your spouse, to a trust for her or a partnership of which she is a member, to minor children or grandchildren, or to a corporation controlled by or for your spouse or such minors, the spread between your depreciated basis for the property and the sales price you get will be treated as ordinary income; not as capital gain. That's because the buyers will have a higher depreciation deduction based on what they paid for the property and a special section of the Internal Revenue Code blocks that kind of deal. But you can still arrange things so that you get the higher depreciation deduction for the family by simply selling the property to *adult* children or grandchildren, or to a corporation controlled by them. You can almost certainly get the same benefits by selling to a *trust* for minor children or grandchildren, since the statute does not expressly reach transactions for their accounts except when the buyer is a corporation.

If you sell to one of the prohibited purchasers, ordinary income tax on the spread between your depreciated basis and the sales price you get for the property takes all the family benefit out of the deal. But if you sell to adult children or grandchildren, a corporation controlled by them or a trust for their benefit, your gain is capital gain on which you pay a maximum 25-35% tax and they still get the higher depreciation deduction.

Sometimes the results are fantastic. Assume you have a business property that cost $50,000 and that you've been depreciating at $2,500 a year for ten years. If it's now worth $125,000 and has a remaining useful life of twenty years, a new buyer can get $6,250 a year depreciation, so he pays income taxes on $3,750 less rental income than you do. On a sale for $125,000, you'd have $100,000 gain, $25,000 tax. If your adult son bought the property from you for $125,000, he could look forward to $100,000 more depreciation (and that means tax-exempt rent) over the next twenty years than you could get— $37,500 more for the first ten years—during which you still can depreciate at $2,500 a year; then $62,500 for the next ten-year period, during which you could have depreciated nothing. His increased depreciation deduction amortizes your capital gain tax for the family as a whole in something like six and one-third years.

Selling Your Business

Sometimes it makes very good sense to sell your business to your adult children or even to trusts for your minor children. It can be done, even though they don't have the money to pay for it in full. If you're dealing with adults who are active in the business, the three main approaches are the installment sale, the contingent sale and the annuity sale.

Under the installment sale you negotiate the price and set the terms of payment at so much down and so much per year until the remaining balance and any interest you may have specified and agreed upon are both paid off. If you set the terms so that you get no more than 30% of the purchase price in the first year, you can treat the sale as a casual installment sale and treat each payment as you get it as a partial return of your cost or other basis and a partial realization of gain. So, if you invested $100,000 and sell out for $200,000—$40,000 down and $20,000 a year for eight years—you don't have to treat the deal as a closed transaction under which you got $200,000 for your $100,000 property and so realized a $100,000 gain taxable in that year. Instead, you apportion the $40,000 you get as a first installment between recovery of your basis and realized gain. Because your basis represents one-half of the sale price, you treat one-half as a return of your basis and one-half as taxable long-term gain.

To make an installment sale of this kind stick for tax purposes, you'd better not take demand notes. Their fair market value would have to be included in your income in the year of sale and that would defeat the objective of allocating the installments only as you get them. You have to use an installment sale contract—under which any security that is given to you is not immediately marketable by you—and so cannot be reduced to value in your hands in the year in which you close the deal.

You can handle a sale of this kind in such a way that you don't take any gain into account until after you've got back your investment or basis in the business. That's what the contingent sale does. Under it, you can specify—if we assume the same figures as in the previous example—payment of $40,000 down and payment of such a percentage of the average normal net income of the business (or whatever other standard you choose to use, such as gross sales, or net income after adding back salaries drawn by the buyers or any number of other variants) as would normally work out to an acceptable annual payment over an agreed upon term. [20]

You can go further, too, and specify that the total amount paid over the term must be at least equal to $200,000, or else payments must be continued until that minimum amount has been paid. Under a deal of this sort all the payments you get are first applied against your basis and are received tax-free until you get your basis back. After that, all the payments are treated as long-term capital gain on which your maximum tax is 25%.[21] That's because this is another "open" transaction and the courts have said that you just don't know when or if you are going to get the full purchase price, because its payment is contingent on the performance of the business. Therefore the value of the sales contract cannot be pegged accurately enough for capital gains tax to lie at the time the deal is consummated.

------

[20] *When a close corporation is involved in a contingent sale like this, and certain family members . . . such as children, grandchildren, spouse or parents . . . also own stock in the corporation, the sale cannot be made to the corporation itself without danger that the installments will be taxed as dividends. In that situation, sell to the other stockholders as individuals—or use the non-contingent installment method described above—or the private annuity described later in this chapter.*

[21] *At the rate of payment, capital gain in any one year is well under $50,000.*

The Private Annuity Sale

Probably the most interesting arrangement to use within the family group is the private annuity sale. Assume the $200,000 sale price and $100,000 basis figures that we used before. Then, on the private annuity method, your boys would buy your business and would agree to pay you for it at the rate of so many dollars a year for as long as you live without any floor or any ceiling on the payments. The actual payments could be pegged at the amount you could get by using $200,000 to buy a like annuity from a commercial insurance company. They could be set somewhat higher on the theory that all the value goes to annuity income and none to sales or administrative expense. If you are in normal health, the safest course is to use the official tables published by the U.S. Treasury. If you are either in impaired health or come from abnormally long-lived stock, the payments could be worked out by an actuary using appropriate medical data and recognized annuity tables with the appropriate adjustments and interest assumptions. The important thing is that the payments have an established actuarial relationship to the purchase price they represent.

As long as the purchase price of the business represents its fair market value, you aren't making any gifts to the buyers. As long as the amount they agree to pay you each year represents the amount that a commercial insurance company would pay had you bought an annuity for a consideration equal to the fair market value of your business . . . or the payments have a sensible actuarial relationship to that price . . . their payments are not gifts to you. The transaction is another "open" one, so you don't treat the entire purchase price as received in the year in which you close the sale. Instead you treat each payment as you get it as annuity income. That means that part of each payment is taxable to you as ordinary income and part of it is tax-exempt. The tax-exempt part of each payment applies against your basis or investment in the business—in our example, $100,000. After you have gotten back the $100,000, you start treating the tax-exempt part of the annuity payments as long-term capital gain and you pay long-term capital gain tax on it until you have received $100,000 gain. After that, all the annuity income is taxed once again as annuity income—part of it taxable and part of it exempt for the rest of your life.[22]

The children don't do so badly either. They cannot take a deduction for the annuity income they pay you because it represents an installment on the purchase price of a capital asset; but they do stand to buy the business awfully cheap if you don't live for very long. If you have a long life and they pay out more than $200,000, each payment made in excess of that amount is added to their cost basis and will be recoverable tax-free when they sell in their turn. If you die before they've paid out very much, they've had a bargain and your estate has saved the estate tax on the spread between what they have paid you and the value of the business. That spread doesn't give them a taxable windfall in the year of your death either. It simply gives them a low basis for the business, so they'll have that much more capital gain if they sell. But the chances are that they won't sell, and even if they do they can get around some of the capital gain.

For instance, if they bought stock from you, they could sell assets instead of stock and their low cost for the stock would not affect their gain on the assets. They'd simply have a corporate shell with cash instead of other assets in it and could put that cash to work in another business. It's more likely, though, that they would hang on and bequeath their stock to their children. Then the values at the dates of their deaths would control and establish their children's basis for determining gain or loss on subsequent sale of that stock. The annuity deal is not used much by the young; but those well along in the sixties or seventies often find it suits their needs. The chances are very good in that age bracket that the seller won't live long enough to get the full purchase price in the form of annuity payments, so substantial estate tax-saving usually results. The seller's income tax is pleasantly affected, too, because the amount of annuity income he gets is probably somewhat greater than the dividend income or partnership share he would have gotten

---

[22] *In a questionable ruling the IRS has attempted to tax the gain differently by allowing cost recovery out of the taxable portion of the annuity income, treating that portion as capital gain after cost recovery and until recovery of sale price and then taxing it as ordinary income. The effect is to deny use of the gain upon sale of the property as part of the cost of the annuity. It seems to be wrong, but we must await court decision to be sure.*

had there been no sale. And the annuity income is partially tax-exempt in contrast with the fully taxable nature of dividends or partnership earnings.

Here are two examples in tabular form:

Stipulated purchase price: $200,000. Seller: male aged 70. Method of payment: immediate life annuity at Mutual Benefit rates, first payment due one year after closing and annually thereafter; last payment, that due for the period prior to that in which death occurs. Basis of property: $100,000. Market value on date of sale: $200,000.

A. The Traditional Treatment

Year	Total Annual Payment	Nontaxable Basis Recovery Annual	Cum.	Taxable Capital Gain Annual	Cum.	Excludible Annuity Income	Taxable Ordinary Income
1	$28,976	$16,528	$16,528	—		—	$12,4
6	$28,976	$16,528	$99,168	—		—	$12,4
7	$28,976	832	100,000	$15,696	$15,696	—	$12,4
8	$28,976	—	100,000	$16,528	$32,224	—	$12,4
12	$28,976	—	100,000	$16,528	$98,336	—	$12,4
13	$28,976	—	100,000	1,664	100,000	$14,864	$12,4
14	$28,976	—	100,000	—	100,000	$16,528	$12,4

B. The New Treasury Approach

Year	Total Annual Payment	Taxable Capital Gain	Cumulative Capital Gain	Excludible Annuity Income	Taxable Ordinary Income
1	$28,976	$8,264	$8,264	$8,264	$12,448
2	$28,976	$8,264	$16,258	$8,264	$12,448
12	$28,976	$8,264	$99,168	$8,264	$12,448
13	$28,976	832	100,000	$8,264	$19,880
14	$28,976	—	100,000	$8,264	$20,712

If the property you've sold the children is depreciable property, they can't wait until your death has established the actual amount they have paid under the annuity arrangement to establish a final basis. They need a basis immediately so they can compute depreciation. For that purpose, the sale price—or fair market value of the property, where that is the purchase price—is taken as the value of the prospective annuity payments. When the deal has not been made at arm's length, they use the actuarial value of the prospective annuity payments rather than the recited purchase price. Probably, if the purchase price called for is higher than fair market value . . . so that there's an element of gift running from the buyers to the seller . . . the buyer's basis would be reduced accordingly; if the recited purchase price was lower than the fair market value of the property . . . so that there was an element of gift from the seller to the buyer . . . the buyer's basis would be the actuarial value of the prospective annuity payments plus that part of the seller's basis for the entire property that represents the ratio of the value of the gift to the total value of the property.

Sometimes the buyer decides to sell the property while he is still obligated to pay the annuity. When that happens, fairly elaborate rules come into play to establish whether he has made a gain, a loss, or a stand-off on the entire transaction. To calculate the amount of gain, if any, the buyer compares the price he receives for the property with a special basis equal to the amount he has paid in annuity to the date of sale plus the value of future annuity installments he's still obligated to make. To compute the amount of his loss, if any, he compares the price received for the property with the total annuity payments made up to the time of sale.

Sometimes such a sale produces neither a loss nor a gain. That would be the case when the amount received for the property was greater than the total annuity payments made up to that time but less than those annuity payments plus the value of the annuities yet to be paid. Then there is no gain because the sale price is less than the annuity payments that have actually been made and the value of those remaining to be paid; and there is no loss because the amount actually paid prior to the sale of the property is less than the price received on that sale.

After the buyer has sold the property, he may still realize gain or loss because of his continuing payment of the annuity obligation. If a gain was recognized upon the sale of the property, annuity payments, in addition to the basis used in computing the gain, are deductible. If a loss is recognized on the sale, all further annuity payments are deductible. If neither gain nor loss was recognized on the sale, no loss is realized until the annuity payments exceed the selling price. The buyer may realize gain, too, after he has sold the property. That would come about if the total annuity payments actually made, as of the date of the seller's death, proved to be less than the basis used in reporting the gain on the sale of the property. It could happen, too, when the sale of the property produced neither gain nor loss and the seller dies at a time when the total annuity payments made by the buyer are less than the selling price of the property. Under these conditions, the gain is taxable to the buyer in the year of the seller's death.

It's because of these complicated rules that come into play when the buyer of property for an annuity sells that property while he is still obligated to make annuity payments, that the private annuity doesn't seem to lend itself too well to security transactions within the family. Too many pressures call for trading in securities—and trading would bring these rules into play. But the stock of a family corporation is not the sort of security that is apt to be bought and sold in order to ride with the market; investment real estate is not apt to be sold lightly and this kind of asset fits ideally into the private annuity concept. It does so because it's the kind of asset that normally you want to keep within the family and it is also the kind of asset that has limited marketability combined with high value so that you want to get it out of the estate in order to avoid embarrassing valuation and liquidity problems.

The mere fact that you sell your business to your children doesn't mean that you have to retire and gather barnacles. You can sell the business and still take an employment contract for a period of years or for the rest of your life and get your contract pay in addition to the purchase price installments on the sale. Probably that's the sort of arrangement you would want to make because it would give you a chance to keep busy, keep an eye on this investment that you're selling on a contingent basis, and give the buyers the benefit of your experience and acumen in the business. If you would not want the business to come back to you upon a failure of a son's obligation to pay your annuity because he predeceased you, you could arrange for him to carry enough insurance on his life in your favor to make up the amount of his annuity obligation. Then his share of the business could go down to his widow or his children and your pay-out would be unaffected.

Care Is Indicated

It's worth repeating and emphasizing and repeating again: Transactions within the family are looked at much more sternly . . . much more closely . . . than transactions with strangers. That doesn't mean that you cannot safely make them. It does mean that they must be at least as formal as transactions with strangers. Use written contracts, written agreements, written instruments. Be certain that the transfers are true and real and that the new owners have actual control of the property. When the new owners are a spouse or minor children or adult children in a vastly inferior capacity, be sure to use an independent corporate trustee, because he will give substance and validity to the transaction. He must, by law, do everything in the best interests of his trust beneficiaries, whether that is in your best interest or not; so he is your best protection against the transaction being set aside as a mere tax sham. Whenever deductible payments are to be made within the family group, be certain that they are made within two and one-half months after the close of the payor's tax year. They should be made in cash, but can be made by demand note or constructively by placing the required amounts to the unrestricted credit of the payee; otherwise an accrual basis payor will not get a deduction for amounts payable to a cash basis payee. If actual or constructive payment in satisfactory form is made within the two and one-half months, the payor will get his deduction. Here the rule is much more rigid than when the payee is a stranger, so even more formality than would ordinarily be indicated must be observed.

The Family Business

The family business is in the form of a proprietorship, partnership, corporation or unincorporated association of some sort. The actual form it has taken may have been adopted by chance or may have been deliberately chosen after full consideration of the advantages and compensating disadvantages inherent in each separate form of organization. Whatever the basis of the choice, however, periodic checks on its continuing desirability make sense. Changes in tax rates can make it advantageous to shift from corporation to partnership or vice versa. Changes in the economy and in the growth trend of the particular business may make a change in the form of doing business advantageous. Technical tax and accounting considerations may provide sufficient immediate tax benefits to justify such a change. Changes in family circumstances, in health of family members, drastic reworking of your estate plan all may dictate a change from one form of doing business to another. There are no absolute rules of thumb. Questions of business policy, legal liability, tax status, the character and quality of the business and the makeup of the family group all pertain and must be studied. The final decision must be made after consultation with competent legal and technical authority whose recommendations are based upon such studies. This is a job for your attorney and your accountant; but it is a job well worth doing and one that can easily result in substantial recoveries of income, substantial increases in estate value and sound integration of your business or its fair capital value with the rest of your estate.

Why all the fuss and feathers? Why periodic studies of something well established and in successful operation? How can the income yield of the business be affected by the fact that it is a corporation or a partnership? Let's just take a look:

Let's assume that you are a proprietor now and that you decide to take your children into business with you, giving each of them a one-third partnership interest in your firm, but that you retain 50% of the partnership income yourself — half as compensation for your services and half as a return on your capital. That means that you're splitting half of the future partnership income three ways. You can't do this one month before the end of the year and make more than one-half of one-twelfth of that year's income taxable to them. If the two-thirds capital interest you give the children would have been taxed at a 30% rate in your estate at your death and if the children's partnership income and the tax-savings developed by taking them into partnership are accumulated at 2-1/2% compound interest, the results can be astounding.

On the premise that the net business income is the net taxable income because deductions and exemptions are just equal to income from other sources, the tax savings at various levels of business income would be:

Net Business Income	Proprietor's Tax	Family Partners' Taxes	Yearly Saving
$ 25,000	$ 6,020	$ 4,897	$ 1,123
50,000	16,940	12,426	4,514
75,000	30,470	22,490	7,980
100,000	45,180	25,994	19,236
200,000	110,980	88,828	22,152
250,000	145,980	103,420	42,560

Even without the effect of compound interest, the savings mount materially over periods of ten, fifteen or twenty years. To give effect to 2½% compound interest after taxes on those savings, simply multiply the yearly saving effected by the creation of the family partnership by 1.280085 for ten years, 1.448298 for fifteen years of 1.638616 for twenty years. To get a true picture of the addition to family wealth, you must add the estate tax saved on the value of the partnership interest given to your children after due allowance for the gift tax that may have had to be paid, properly weighted with interest.

Family Partnerships

Family partnerships may be created by giving partnership interests to your children or other members of the family or by selling such interests to them. If your business is a personal service business in which capital is not a material income-producing factor, the family partnership is not for you unless the child or other relative you are going to take in can be expected to perform services on an important and regular basis. Then his partnership interest is an interest in the earnings of the personal service partnership to which he has contributed valuable services.

But if your partnership is one in which capital is important, such as a retail business, a manufacturing company or such, you may give a capital interest to a relative. It must be an honest-to-goodness gift so that the partnership interest is fully transferred to the relative and you no longer have any rights in it. The donee must be able to withdraw his capital interest and must be entitled to its value on withdrawal or on liquidation of the partnership and he must be entitled to the income too.

That doesn't mean that the partnership agreement cannot provide for you—or for someone else—to act as managing partner; or for you to have a first refusal on the family member's partnership interest when he does want to sell, because those are perfectly normal restrictions that can be found in thousands of nonfamily partnership arrangements. But the facts must show clearly that your donee is a partner in fact and that he, or his fiduciary, if he is a minor, is entitled to the appropriate share of the partnership income and has normal freedom of action as to the disposition of both his capital interest in the partnership and his share of the income.

An example of the kind of thing that goes to the reality of the partnership arrangement and that demonstrates that no real partnership was actually intended is the gift of a partnership interest in all the assets of a manufacturing business except for plant and equipment which have been retained by the former proprietor and leased to the partnership. While such an arrangement might not affect the realities of the partnership where your partners were adult or active in the business and perfectly capable of taking care of their own interests, it would most certainly cast doubt where your partners were inactive minors whose income interests could be seriously affected by the way in which you chose to handle the underlying assets essential to the operation of the partnership business.

Then, too, when a partnership interest is given or sold to a family member who is not active in the business, its effectiveness in transferring taxable partnership income to the new partner is limited to a fair return on his capital interest after the partnership income has been charged with fair compensation for the services of the working partners. Even then, that part of the partnership income attributable to the capital interests of the inactive family members may not be proportionately greater than that part attributable to the capital interest of the donor. And for the purpose of this test a sale to an inactive partner who is a member of the immediate family group (spouse, children, parents, brothers and sisters, trusts for their benefit, etc.) is treated exactly like a gift.

So long as his right to withdraw or otherwise deal with his partnership interest is not restricted to an unusal degree, a donee will be recognized as a limited partner, so it is perfectly feasible to establish trusts for minor children and give them limited partnership interests. Then the trustee can take active part in the councils of the partnership and in the management of the partnership business and so prepare himself to carry on after the death of the former proprietor and until his wards are capable of assuming full partnership status in their own right.

Sometimes it's more practical to sell a partnership interest to children or other relatives. Such a sale can be for cash or on the cuff with the purchase price to be paid out of the earnings of the partnership interest itself. For such a sale to be treated as a legitimate transaction—and not merely as a sham intended to produce income tax savings without material change in the economic position of the seller—it is necessary to show either that the sale was actually intended to promote the interest of the business by securing the active business participation of the buyer or (and this is the important consideration where minors or inactive family members are the buyers) that the terms of sale—especially in regard to credit, security, interest rates and such—are those of an arm's length transaction and might reasonably be expected to be acceded to by a stranger.

Family Corporations

Corporations are somewhat easier to handle and the division of corporate income amongst members of the family group can be accomplished a little more freely. Gifts of stock are not surrounded by the restrictions and the regulations that relate to gifts of partnership interests. Sales of stock at full value are not treated as though they were gifts. Maybe the reason is that the

corporation is a separate entity distinct and apart from its stockholders and with income of its own. It follows that employees of
the corporation are paid for their services, even though they be
stockholders, since salaries are deductible expenses and the
greater the amount that can be allocated to reasonable salary
payments, the lower the corporation tax base. That makes it
unnecessary to guard against an artificial diversion of income of
the sort that would be possible in a family partnership arrangement.

At any rate, whatever the reasons, the law is a lot more lenient
in regard to gifts or sales of corporate stock to relatives and the
dividends on such stock are treated as taxable income to the
owners of the shares, no matter how they acquired those shares
and no matter how shortly after that acquisition the dividend is
declared. Well, if you want to limit your dividend income from
your *new* corporation, you can do it by providing for an issue of
preferred stock calling for a guaranteed dividend that will use up
most of the amount distributable in dividends. Then that
preferred stock can be put in trust and the result will be an
accumulation of distributable corporate earnings in a tax shelter
in which they will be subject to lower rates of tax than if you were
to receive them yourself. If you face the problem with an existing
corporation that has accumulated surplus, a better way is to
issue a second class of common stock entitled to dividends before
any are paid on the original (or other) common.

A partner is an employer, not an employee; but a stockholder-
officer of a corporation is an employee. If your business is
incorporated, then you, as an officer-employee, may participate
in a qualified pension trust or profit-sharing trust established for
the corporation's employees. You will share in the trust benefits
on the same basis as any other employee—usually in direct
proportion to salary and length of service. Because it is usual for
the stockholder-officers to have the longest tenure and the
highest salaries, they generally get the lion's share of the benefits
from a tax-exempt employee's trust. This simply means that they
get the benefit of a substantial sum of corporate money accumulated for them in a tax shelter and eventually turned over to them
at preferential rates, if the cash value of their interests is paid out

to them within one taxable year because of a severance of employment, such as at death or retirement.

Here's an example of how stockholder-employees and their families can benefit from a profit-sharing trust, assuming that the corporation contributes the maximum deductible amount— 15% of the salary of the participating employees each year—and completely ignoring the effects of interest:

Suppose that three stockholders, A, B, and C, draw $20,000 salary each; that employee D, who is the son of stockholder A, draws $9,000; and that the total salary for fifteen ordinary employees aggregates $60,000. Total payroll, then, comes to $129,000 and the maximum deductible contribution to the profit-sharing trust is $19,350. On this basis, the stockholders and the son are credited with $10,350 out of the total contribution; only $9,000 goes to the credit of the fifteen other employees.

Now, if the corporation did not contribute the $19,350 and so was unable to deduct it from its taxable income, it would have to pay 48% tax and would net only $10,062 to add to surplus or distribute in dividends. Added to surplus, the $10,062 would be beyond the reach of the stockholders . . . unless they sell their stock and so realize the surplus as capital gain . . . or unless they choose to declare a dividend. If the $10,062 were paid out in dividends, it would probably be taxed at a 50% rate because dividend and investment income added to a $20,000 salary could easily reach that level. If it were subject to a 50% tax rate, the stockholders would net, as a group, only $5,031 out of the $19,350 chunk of corporate earnings. Compare that with the $10,350 placed to their credit in the profit-sharing trust and with the net $8,844 that their $10,350 profit-sharing trust allocation produces after an income tax based upon ten times the tax upon one-tenth of the distribution upon retirement or death and made in a single year in which income other than salary equals all deductions and exemptions.

But the equity owners' benefits don't stop there. Forfeitures can be and usually are built into profit-sharing trusts, so that employees cannot take the contributions made for them when they quit unless they have been employed for a specified number of years. For instance, it's common practice to stagger the "vested" portion of an employee's profit-sharing account so that he takes none of it with him if he quits during the first five years and can take away only a specified percentage of his allocation for each year of service after that. A usual and quite fair formula is no vesting for the first five years, then 50% vesting, plus 10% additional per year after five years, with the result that ten years' service vests the employee fully. Forfeited profit shares are left in the trust and are divided up among those people who stay until death, disability or retirement, so you can see that the chance of the forfeitures benefiting the stockholders and their families are very good indeed. The end result is that a tax-sheltered profit-sharing trust can easily give the stockholders and their families 15% of their salaries, plus a very substantial percentage of the amounts forfeited by employees who quit too soon, plus substantial interest earnings on both.

Partners and Proprietors May Have More Limited Pension or Profit Sharing Plans

In contrast, partners and proprietors may also participate in qualified plans as employees but on a more restricted basis. Only their earned income from the business, as opposed to their shares of yield upon capital investment, is treated as "compensation" for contribution purposes, so an inactive partner or proprietor cannot participate. However, a partner or proprietor who does perform personal services treats *all* income from his business as personal earnings or compensation. He may contribute the greater of $7,500 or 15% of these earnings to a qualified plan for his own benefit. Other requirements must be met for regular employees, no forfeitures may occur and the arrangement is far less pleasing than a like one for a corporation; but you may find it useful especially if you have only a few long-term employees or no employees who are apt to be with you for as long as three years.

Electing, or Sub-Chapter S, Corporations

One of the reasons proprietors and partners used to have for not incorporating was the added expense of the corporation income tax. Now they can incorporate and elect not to pay corporate taxes but, instead, to treat the net or undistributed taxable income of the corporation as their own and pay personal tax on it just as if they had remained proprietors or partners. The major advantages are the limited liability for business debts that a corporation offers and, up to now, the chance to participate in qualified pension and profit-sharing plans as employees, because stockholder-officers *are* corporate employees. To enjoy this benefit, the corporation must have ten or fewer stockholders all of whom are natural persons or the estates of deceased natural persons (no trusts) and all of whom are resident in the United States and consent to the election to not pay corporate taxes.

Qualified employee plan benefits for five percent or greater stockholders—called shareholder-employees—of a Subchapter S corporation are broader than for partners and proprietors, but more limited than those for stockholder-employees of regularly taxable corporations. For example, such shareholder-employees may not benefit by forfeitures under profit-sharing plans and any employer contribution greater than the smaller of $7,500 or 15% of compensation made for such a shareholder-employee is currently taxed to him as compensation and recoverable by him tax-free upon receipt of his benefits at death, retirement, or severance of employment.

The two major problems that must be faced by the owner of the business when he wants to tie that business interest into the rest of the estate are: Shall I try to retain my business for my family? Or shall I sell it and realize its capital value for reinvestment for the family?

Retention For The Family

Whether a business should be retained depends upon many factors. Obviously, retention isn't worth while if the business cannot be relied upon to produce a reasonable level of income with or without a fair chance of capital appreciation. It certainly can't be retained if successor management doesn't exist or cannot be found and provided adequate working capital. Even if the business is productive, successor management is available, and working capital is adequate, attempts to retain the business for the family are doomed to failure unless it can be protected against the in-roads of estate taxes and other transfer costs. The estate must have or must be provided with enough liquid cash to pay the costs of transfer and the taxes payable at death without having to look to the business or to the sale of the business in order to raise the money, else retention is just a pleasant but unrealizable dream.

Sometimes checking all these aspects of whether retention of the business is worth while brings us to the conclusion that we can retain only part. This may be because we must sell part to raise sufficient money to pay the costs of dying, or it may be because successor management has to be given a proprietory interest in order to provide the incentives for successful operation. When that is the case, the retention of a preferred stock interest in a corporation—or a limited partnership interest in a partnership business—may still offer very great advantage to the family or the heirs. The risk of capital loss is minimized in both preferred stock and limited partnership interests, because a stop-loss is put at the amount left at risk in the business, with the rest of the estate held separate and apart from that, and because both types of investment interests enjoy preferred positions on liquidation of the business.

They get first call on what is left after creditors have been discharged. They get first call on income, too, and, since sound estate planning would not consider the retention of even a preferred stock or a limited partnership interest in a business that was not soundly established and had not stood the test of time, that preference as to earnings is valuable. It provides an important method of averaging up the income of the estate and providing a familiar and seasoned equity investment for the family. When you stop to consider that it is often possible to limit the retained preferred stock or limited partnership interest to that part of the value of your business that is over and above its net worth or liquidating value, so that the only money at risk represents the potential but not yet realized intangible values, the estate planning advantage is emphasized.

Disposing of The Business

When the decision is to dispose of the business or the business interest either at death or retirement, three related problems must be faced and solved. First, a market must be established so that the transaction may take place at the planned time and on a planned basis. Second, adequate financing must be provided so that the market will function efficiently and the transaction will be consummated with at least a sufficient initial cash payment to provide the liquid funds needed by the estate and to minimize the possibility of loss through failure to realize the balance of the purchase price because of subsequent failure of the business itself. Third, the instruments of transfer must be so arranged as to establish the price at which the interest passes hands as controlling for estate tax valuation purposes.

The market for any business or business interest is usually composed of co-stockholders, co-partners, employees or competitors. In that order, they represent those best able to benefit from the acquisition of additional equity interests and from the opportunity to own and control the business. To the extent that shareholders, partners or employees are either inactive or incapable of assuming management, the group of natural purchasers shrinks.

Active partners and co-stockholders are the most logical buyers because the preservation of their own active employment is involved. Employees of management calibre, or employees as a large group represented by a pension trust or a profit-sharing trust, are logical purchasers for much the same reason.

Inactive co-owners whose interests are almost entirely those of investors are more logically sellers than buyers since the security of the silent, or pure investment, interest is tied to the continuation of the enterprise and that, in turn, depends upon continued successful management. Competitors are usually interested only in a bargain price since their concern is to garner a larger part of the market for their products or services, whether that be by the elimination of competition or by its absorption. Yet competitors at times offer the best market, especially when they make it possible to merge a closely held business with a larger publicly held one whose shares are quoted on the securities markets.

A market is no better than its financing or than the ability of the purchasers to pay. Shareholders, co-partners, employees may all to a greater or lesser degree use the earning power and resources of the business itself to fund their purchase obligation. As to stockholders and partners, this is self-evident whenever the corporation has accumulated surplus that may be used for the redemption of stock or the partnership has substantial and reasonably liquid capital reserves that can be used to pay out a retiring partner's capital interest. As to employees, it is evident when one considers the possibility of increasing the salaries of certain selected employees so that they may purchase insurance on the lives of stockholders or partners in order to fund their personal contractual obligations to purchase the shareholdings or partnership interests. It is evident, too, when the purchase is made on their behalf by a tax-exempt pension trust or profit-sharing trust.

In the first instance, the salary increases, if reasonable for the services actually rendered, are deductible business expenses and so enable the employees to benefit by a large proportion of the corporate or partnership income tax dollar which has been diverted to them in the form of salary. This tends to result in an opportunity for them to acquire an ownership interest at a cost roughly equal to the personal income tax they would have to pay on the increased compensation. In the case of the tax-exempt trust, of course, the pattern is even clearer because the total diversion from corporate or partnership income tax to trust contribution is available for equity purchase purposes. Time is essential when business reserves or trust accumulations are to provide the total purchase price of the equity interest; but life insurance purchases time, and the devotion of some part of the funding to the payment of premiums on the life of the seller of the equity interest will provide the necessary cash at the time it is needed and at the cost of a relatively few cents on the ultimate purchasing dollar.

Estate tax valuation is always at fair market. Thus all factors going to value must be taken into account. Among them are book value, capitalized value of earnings, dividends, liquidating value of corporate assets, capitalized value of superior earning power (reflecting intangibles, such as management performance, goodwill and such), the value of the services rendered to the business by the deceased owner and the value of comparable businesses which have been sold upon the open market at some recent point in time. Of these various factors, book value and dividends are the least reliable indices because book value places major emphasis upon accounting practices and so may reflect distortions of true value; dividend history is merely a distorted picture of dividend-paying capacity. The controlling factor, where statistics are available, is the price at which comparable business interests have changed hands on the open market. As to publicly held corporations, the statistics are to be found in the records of the various securities exchanges; as to close corporations, partnership and proprietorship interests, through the testimony of business brokers specializing in that area. A method commonly used by the Internal Revenue Service and practical for the use of business owners who are seeking to establish fair market value for their own contract purposes is the application of a formula that combines asset value and capitalization of superior earning power. Ordinarily, the formula treats between 6% and 30% of asset value as normal return on capital, depending upon the stability or hazardousness of the particular business, and calls for capitalization of the excess of average earnings for a normal five- or ten-year period at somewhere between 20% and 50% to produce the capitalized value of the intangibles. The sum of asset value and the capitalized value of the intangibles after application of the formula is, of course, the fair market value of the business itself. A good rule-of-thumb as to the percentage to be allowed as a normal return on capital is to use the industry average, since that would take into account stability . . . the relative importance of working capital . . . the fragility of goodwill . . . and the time lag between investment and realization of profit.

Purely by way of example, a stable department store might well be assumed to return 8% on invested capital and to justify capitalization of superior earnings at 20%, which represents five years' purchase; but the far more hazardous heavy construction business requiring substantial investments in earthmoving equipment and in payroll might well be expected to return between 20% and 30% on invested capital and to capitalize its superior earnings at between 50% and 100%—the equivalent of one or two years' purchase. The important thing is not so much what precise valuation factors have been used as the fact that consideration has been given to intangible values as well as to invested capital and that the application of the formula has produced fair market value at the time of execution of the purchase and sale contract. The courts have held that a binding purchase and sale contract will peg the estate tax value of the interest subject to the contract at the purchase price called for, provided that: 1. the seller is committed as to sales during life as well as at death; 2. effect has been given to the value of the intangibles; and 3. the dollar purchase price specified represents fair market value when the contract was entered into or that the formula specified is reasonable and will tend to produce a figure reasonably close to fair market value at the time the contract is performed.

Not all such arrangements call for the payment of the entire purchase price in cash; nor is it necrssary that the contract become effective and that performance under it be completed only after the death of the seller. It is often desirable to sell one's business interest at retirement, rather than to wait until death. It is often desirable to sell on some basis other than for cash, either because of the inability of the buyers to produce the total purchase price at one time, or because of the desirability of retaining an interest in the enterprise for one's estate or one's heirs.

Income Tax Aspects

Sales at death present some new capital gain tax problems, since the Tax Reform Act of 1976 now provides that the basis for determination of gain upon a sale of property by an estate or an heir is the basis of the decedent adjusted to reflect value on December 31, 1976, and further increased by any transfer—*i.e.,* estate or gift—tax paid. It seems inevitable that the law provides a built-in capital gain liability—negligible in the early years following 1976 but of increasing dimensions thereafter.

This is true to an even greater degree in the case of a sale during life because at that time the basis of the seller for determining gain or loss is the adjusted cost of his business interest and any spread is taxed as long-term capital gain if he has held that interest for more than nine months.

Now, there's a vast difference between paying a 25%-35% capital gains tax on a substantial amount of gain that has been realized in cash—so that the money to discharge the tax is at hand—and paying such a tax when only a portion of the purchase price (and hence of the gain) has been realized in cash and the balance has been received merely in the form of marketable obligations having delayed maturity dates. So it becomes wise to consider the various ways in which installment sales can be handled in order to defer the impact of capital gains tax and to select the most advantageous manner of payment.

If the sales price is to be paid in installments over a specified period of time and in a specified amount per installment, it is usually good practice to limit the initial installment payable within the first year to not more than 30% of the total purchase price. That gives the seller an opportunity to treat the sale as a casual sale of personal property and to allocate each installment he receives proportionately between a recovery of his basis and long-term gain. Then a business having a basis of $100,000 in your hands and being sold for $500,000, of which $125,000 is payable immediately and the balance in five equal installments, does not produce $400,000 immediate gain and $100,000 immediate capital gains tax. Instead, the first installment is allocated $31,250 to a return of basis, $93,750 to gain, and, out of that gain, $27,812 to capital gains tax. Each subsequent installment is allocated in similar fashion: one-quarter to recovery of basis and three-quarters to capital gain subject to tax at 25% upon the first $50,000 of gain and 35% upon the rest.

But it may be better business to make the installment purchase payments contingent upon the earning power of the business itself. That can be done by calling for a down payment of $125,000 and annual payments for ten years of a specified percentage of net earnings plus stockholders' salaries with the further proviso that the ten-year payments are to be extended for so long as may be necessary to produce a minimum aggregate $375,000 in addition to the initial $125,000 payment. Then none of the payments received is taxable capital gain until such time as the seller has fully recovered his basis, because their contingent nature makes it impossible to determine when or whether the gain will be realized.

Sometimes it is desirable to maintain a continuing interest in the business, at least for a period of years. Then it may be well to sell for part cash and part preferred stock or limited partnership interest. Under those conditions, the cash payment received upon the sale is first applied against the seller's basis and only the excess is treated as taxable gain. When a partnership interest is sold in part for cash and in part for a limited partnership interest, capital gains tax will lie only on the excess of the cash received over the seller's basis for his partnership interest.

When corporate stock is involved, the rules are much more complex. If cash and preferred stock are received in exchange for common, gain is recognized to the extent of the excess of the cash received over a cost or basis for the common determined by allocating the total cost or basis to the common and preferred shares in proportion to their value. For example, using the figures set out above, the $500,000 price could be taken $250,000 in preferred stock and $250,000 in cash. Half the $100,000 basis would be allocated to each of the common and the preferred, so the recognized gain would be $200,000 ($250,000 cash less $50,000 allocated basis for the common) and the continuing basis for the preferred would be $50,000. Since all of the shareholders' common stock is redeemed and they no longer have power to vote or control, there is no danger of the redemption being viewed as a dividend distribution—or as anything other than a sale of the block of common stock to the corporation itself. Unless family members own common stock which is attributable to them under the statute, the amount received in payment for the common stock will be treated as capital gain to the extent that it exceeds the allocated basis for the common stock.

But if family members do own stock in the corporation, competent counsel must be sought out because stock redemption is then apt to be tricky. To avoid easy withdrawal of corporate surplus at capital gains rates instead of the ordinary rates applying to dividend distributions, the law treats corporate distributions in redemption of stock as dividends unless:

1. The distribution is not essentially equivalent to a dividend—that is, it results in a marked change in the degree of control and the economic relationship of the stockholder to the corporation, or

2. The distribution is disproportionate as to the stockholder, so that he ends up after it with: a. less than 50% of the common stock and voting power of the corporation *and* b. the voting or common stock he holds after the redemption has a ratio to the common then outstanding that is less than 80% the ratio borne by his holdings before redemption to the then outstanding voting or common stock, or

3. His entire interest in the corporation, other than as mere creditor, is terminated by the redemption, or

4. A partial redemption is made after death to produce not more than the sum of the death taxes, funeral expense and administration expense charged against the estate. Even then, the stock redeemed must be part of a block included in gross estate and having a value equal to 50% of the adjusted gross estate.

Attribution, or When His Is Mine

The problem is that, except in the last situation described in 4 above, stock owned by others may be attributed to a shareholder and treated as though it were his—and that can make it impossible to meet the requirements for disproportionate redemptions or termination of interest. Such "attribution" treats stock as owned by a person when it is actually owned by: a. his parents, spouse, children, or grandchildren; b. an estate or trust of which he is a beneficiary, in proportion to his interest in the estate or trust; c. a corporation of which he holds 50% or more of the stock, in proportion to his stockholdings; or a partnership in which he is a partner, in the proportion of his partnership interest. These rules are complex and no attempt is made to go into them in detail or point out the available counter measures. They are merely mentioned to raise possible danger signals. They can usually be avoided with professional guidance, but are not to be toyed with by anyone other than competent counsel.

Preferred that is taken as a dividend on common or that is issued, as here, in exchange for common stock, will be so-called §306 stock unless the payment of cash instead of the preferred would not have been taxed as a dividend and so as ordinary income. Section 306 stock may not be sold to others or redeemed by the corporation without subjecting the total received for it to ordinary income tax. Before the Tax Reform Act of 1976, the death of the stockholder removed this disability because the preferred stock, as part of his estate, took its value on the estate tax return as its new basis for computing gain or loss on a sale and the law states expressly that then it is no longer *§306* stock. That's why it was wise to hold preferred acquired tax free in exchange for common to be held until the shareholder died and the stock became fully disposable. The new law raises some doubts because of the carryover basis provision—the one that says a decedent's basis carries over to his estate but is adjusted to value on December 31, 1976, and increased by the estate tax paid upon its date of death value. Probably that new provision will *not* have the effect of continuing the *§306* disability because there is no necessary correlation between the two provisions; but we'll have to wait and see. The most likely effect will be preferred stock cleansed of the *§306* imposition of ordinary income (dividend) tax and subject merely to capital gain tax arising under the carryover basis provisions on the excess of par value over the portion of the basis allocated to the preferred from the underlying common stock in respect to which it was issued.

CHAPTER XXI

IF YOU ARE A MIGRANT

Sometimes people marry and live in one state for a lifetime, sometimes they migrate. When such migration takes a couple from a community property state to a non-community property or common law state, it does some violence to the couples' property interests and can create problems in their estate planning. That's true, too, when a couple moves *into* a community property state.

The move in itself does not transform community property into "other" or separate property; nor does it transform previously owned and acquired property into community. What does happen is that the continuity of property characterization is destroyed in most cases: what was community remains so, but what is subsequently acquired is probably separate property *or* what was separate remains so and what is subsequently acquired is community.

The result is that a surviving spouse of such a couple will have different qualitative and quantitative legal rights in the different categories of property acquired during marriage and the deceased will have differing powers and degrees of control of disposition over them. Good counsel and careful planning are at more of a premium than ever.

You see, one cannot dispose of the community property—that is, of one-half of the property acquired during marriage other than by gift or inheritance—owned by one's spouse. So a will does not operate upon that half unless the surviving spouse permits it to do so, refuses to "take against the will." Nevertheless, much sound estate planning is based upon such self-serving acceptance by a survivor who is given income upon the whole community and in exchange gives up only the right to control the flow of her community share upon her subsequent death. Well conceived, such a will forcing the survivor to elect to abide by its terms because she gets more benefit that way, saves considerable estate tax upon the second death and—perhaps even more importantly —provides unified, professional management at least for her life.

This area is mostly too complicated to treat superficially. So here are just a few truly important things to take up with your counsel:

1. When you move *into* a community property state, enter into a formal contract not to be subject to the community property system if that is what you want.

2. When you move *out* of a community property state, enter into a formal contract *either* continuing the community system prevailing since you married *or* agreeing that *future* acquisitions will *not* be part of the community. In this case, be sure that you do *not* have a pre-existing, formal and continuing marriage contract that already binds you. And, if you were married and lived in Louisiana, remember that the fact alone—if you have no other formal, written contract—has subjected you to a continuing marriage contract embodying the community property law—i.e., "the community of acquets and gains"—of Louisiana so that only a formal contract valid under the law of your new domicile will have any chance of suspending the community as to future acquisitions outside of Louisiana.

3. However you move, make sure that formal and written arrangements apply—in addition to mere records of title and such—to property you wish to hold separately, especially if community income is used to maintain or improve it. Examples are bank accounts, life insurance policies, mortgage payments or real estate. Made out of community property, deposits, premiums and payments can transmute separate property gradually into community.

4. Be sure to ask your counsel about how such special doctrines as that of "forced heirship" in Louisiana affect what you *must* leave to your children at your death—whether you moved into or out of that state.

CONCLUSION

Sound estate planning breaks down logically into a series of comparatively simple steps:

1. Determination of the heirs or beneficiaries who will share in the estate.

2. Evaluation of their needs.

3. Separate listing of what the estate owner *hopes* to accomplish for his beneficiaries and what he feels they *must have*.

4. Cold-blooded appraisal of the assets available to meet the needs of the beneficaries and the surplus that may be applied to achieving the aspirations of the estate owner.

5. Careful filling in of the gaps by means of life insurance.

6. Development of a carefully worked out plan of distribution should death occur immediately.

7. Development of a carefully worked out program of investment, accumulation, and intra-family gifts in order to produce the kind of estate required by the end of a reasonable period of time.

8. Development of a practical and sensible plan of education for beneficiaries to prepare them for the kind of lives they will have to lead when the estate owner can no longer be their shield.

9. Careful and complete documentation of all the pertinent facts regarding both the property to be transferred and the people to receive it, so that executors and attorneys do not have to work in the dark.

10. Continuous application of common sense and good practical business judgment so that no obvious exemptions or preferential treatments are overlooked and no unnecessary liabilities are accepted.

One other thing that ought to be stressed is that the day of the lone wolf is over. We are living in too complex a society for any one man, no matter how brilliant, to be able to run all the affairs of his estate without expert guidance. That doesn't mean that an estate owner must not make his own decisions. No one else can make them for him. But he is a blazing fool if, before he jumps at a conclusion, he does not consult competent legal authority, competent insurance authorities, and competent tax and investment counsel. He simply cannot afford to take a chance on ignorance—the cost is much, much too high. So the thing to do is not to consult experts without confiding in them, but to lay one's cards upon the table and to work with the actual facts, figures and situations involved. Then, after a plan has been devised and the estate has been whipped into some sort of respectable shape, the result should be set before those who will be charged with its administration. The executors, the attorneys the estate owner wants them to retain, and even the beneficiaries, should have a clear and unclouded picture of what they will have to face and of the materials with which they will have to work. It may not be quite so flattering as to remain the great man of mystery until the day of death, but it will be lots more satisfying to know what the score really is.

APPENDIX

Perhaps you want to see how your estate can be measured against the needs it *must* satisfy, the extras you want to provide.

These forms were developed by the author for use in estate planning and are reproduced by permission of the copyright holder, The Mutual Benefit Life Insurance Company, Newark, New Jersey. The Estate Organizers develop the information needed to approach the task. The Analysis and Work Sheets put your assets through laboratory probate. They reproduce the job your executor would have to do—paying off debts and taxes and getting down to what you can really dispose of. When that's done, you can begin thinking of who gets what.

Your lawyer, life underwriter, trust officer and accountant will be glad to help.

* * *

ESTATE ORGANIZER FOR PROPERTY PLANNING

ANALYSIS AND WORK SHEETS
FOR PROPERTY PLANNING

Condensed Forms

ESTATE ORGANIZER

FOR

PROPERTY PLANNING

Case No. _____

Name: _____

Date: _____

ESTATE DATA

he Family

	SELF	SPOUSE	CHILDREN AND OTHERS				
RTH DATE							
EGAL RESIDENCE							
EALTH							
THERE A WILL?*							
a. when and where made?							
b. in whose favor?							
c. testamentary trust?							
VING TRUSTS:							
a. created by							
b. in favor of							
c. value							
d. revocable by terms or local law?							
SURANCE TRUSTS:*							
a. created by							
b. value (face of policies)							
c. funded?							
FTS SINCE 6/6/32:							
a. to whom?							
b. when?							
c. value and nature							
d. return filed?*							
NCOME							
a. salary							
b. other							
NHERITANCES (POTENTIAL):							
a. source							
b. worth							
Secure copy.							

NAME AND ADDRESS OF:

Attorney _____

Accountant _____

Physician _____

ESTATE DATA

Assets Schedule

ITEM	CLIENT			SPOUSE			NOTES
	MARKET VALUE	CURRENT YIELD	CONVERSION VALUE	MARKET VALUE	CURRENT YIELD	CONVERSION VALUE	
A. BANK ACCOUNTS sole joint †							
B. U. S. ACCUMULATION BONDS (S, POD, JT †)							
C. GOVERNMENT BONDS							
D. MUNICIPALS							
E. LISTED BONDS							
F. LISTED STOCKS common preferred							
G. UNLISTED BONDS							
H. UNLISTED STOCKS							
I. MORTGAGES							
J. REAL ESTATE sole joint tenancy †							
K. CLOSE CORPORATION STOCK							
L. PARTNERSHIP INTEREST							
M. PROPRIETORSHIP							
N. INTERESTS IN* trusts estates							
O. PERSONAL EFFECTS							
P. LIFE INSURANCE self others on self, owned by others							
Q. ANNUITIES self others							
R. OTHER							
TOTALS	$	$	$	$	$	$	

† List under source of money or purchase price.

* Including Powers of Appointment.

N.B. The value of property held in community should be properly allocated between spouses.

ESTATE DATA

Schedule C

· ·

CLIENT		SPOUSE
	BILLS AND ACCOUNTS PAYABLE	$
	BANK LOANS	
	NOTES PAYABLE	
	INSURANCE BANK LOANS	
	INSURANCE POLICY LOANS	
	BROKERS LOANS	
	MORTGAGES	
	TAXES:	
	real property	
	personal property	
	income	
	other	
	LEASEHOLD LIABILITY: †	
	home	
	business	
	CONTINGENT LIABILITIES:	
	joint notes	
	endorsements (notes, leases, etc.)	
	accounts guaranteed	
	mortgage bonds	
	corporation commitments underwritten ‡	
	partnership liabilities	
	disputed taxes	
	unsettled damages	
	instalment contracts financed	
	other	
		$
	TOTALS	

† Deduct estimated rent from sublet.

‡ Does corporation maintain reserve?

ESTATE DATA

. . . .

1. Retirement at age _____ · financial only _____ ; physical _____

   Income for self and wife: .... $ _____ minimum; $ _____

   Income for survivor: self: .... $ _____ minimum; $ _____

   wife: .... $ _____ minimum; $ _____

2. Estate: (all incomes monthly)

   Income to wife till youngest child is self-supporting: $ _____ minimum; $ _____

   Life income to wife thereafter: .... $ _____ minimum; $ _____

   Special funds:

   Adjustment*: .... $ _____ for _____ for _____

   Education *: .... $ _____ for _____ for _____

   _____ for _____ for _____

   _____ for _____ for _____

   _____ for _____ for _____

   Invasion: .... $ _____ ; annual withdrawal: $ _____ ( ) cun

   ( ) non-cumulative.

   Mortgage cancellation .... $ _____

   Other * † :

NAME	AMOUNT	PURPOSE
_____ $	_____	_____
_____	_____	_____
_____	_____	_____
_____	_____	_____

* Consider trusts, charitable bequests, remainders to charity.
† Consider income and/or capital for children, whether parents live or as remaindermen.

(overleaf for more space)

dditional Data   **Schedule D**

ITEM	NOTES

ESTATE DATA

Corporation   Sche

. . . .

1. Where incorporated: _____ 2. When: _____

3. Nature of business: _____

_____

4. Earnings:
   (Net Before Taxes)

   19___ $ _____ ; 19___ $ _____ ; 19___ $ _____ ; 19___ $ _____

   19___ $ _____ ; 19___ $ _____ ; 19___ $ _____ ; 19___ $ _____
                                                    last three years: last five years:

   19___ $ _____ ; 19___ $ _____ ; $ _____ ; $ _____

5. Book value: _____

6. Capitalization:

	PREFERRED	COMMON	NON-VOTING COMMON	DEBENTURES
Outstanding				
Authorized				
Fixed Dividend or Interest				

7. Funded debt: _____

8. Distribution of shares: self_____; wife_____; children_____; parents_____; other family_____
   unrelated associates_____; trusts_____; estates_____; others_____

9. Purchase-and-sale agreement? _____ With whom? _____ When
   effective: death only? _____ retirement? _____ at any time? _____ Price? _____
   Funding? _____ Mandatory? _____ Recapitalization provisions? _____
   Re-entry for heirs? _____ *(Secure copy of agreement)*

10. Is retention of stock for family desired? _____ Wholly or partially? _____

11. Is any stock under option?_____ To whom?_____ What terms?_____

12. Is executor or trustee directed to retain? _____ To sell? _____ Is will silent? _____ Is
    trust silent? _____

13. Is stock listed? _____ Is stock traded over-the-counter? _____

14. Any recent sales of substantial blocks of stock? _____ Price? _____

15. Any employee benefit plans? _____ Pension? _____ *(Secure copy of plan)*

16. Profit-sharing? _____ How administered _____ *(Secure copy o*

17. Any life insurance on key employees? _____

    (Secure copy of plan)

(overleaf for more space)

. . . .

EM NOTES

ESTATE DATA

Partnership   Sched

. . . .

1. Nature of business: _____

2. Earnings:

    19___ $ _____ ; 19___ $ _____ ; 19___ $ _____ ; 19___ $ _____

    19___ $ _____ ; 19___ $ _____ ; 19___ $ _____ ; 19___ $ _____
                                                 last three years: last five years:

    19___ $ _____ ; 19___ $ _____ ; $ _____ ; $ _____

3. Net worth: _____ 4. Liquidated value: _____

5. Is firm on cash or accrual basis? _____ Taxable year: _____

6. Any receivables not included on last return of partners? _____ Individual's
    share? _____

7. Contingent liabilities? _____ Amount? _____

8. Business continuation agreement? _____ Payments to heirs of deceased? _____
    Stipulated? _____ Ratio of profits? _____ Limited partnership retained for
    heirs? _____

9. Business liquidation agreement? _____ Price? _____ How paid? _____
    Funding? _____

10. Will member of family succeed to interest in firm? _____ On what terms? _____

11. Have you insurance on co-partners' lives? _____ Purpose? _____
    Amount? _____ Cash value? _____

12. Are you insured in favor of co-partners? _____ Purpose? _____
    Amount? _____ Who owns insurance? _____ Cash value? _____

13. Does firm own insurance on co-partners? _____ Purpose? _____
    Amount? _____ Cash value? _____

14. Names of Co-partners: Percentage of Profits and Capital Accounts:

    _____   _____

    _____   _____

    _____   _____

    _____   _____

    _____   _____

15. Any employee benefit plans? _____ Pension? _____ (Secure copy c
    Profit-sharing? _____ How Administered? _____ (Secure copy c

16. Any life insurance on key employees? _____ (Secure copy c

(overleaf for more space)

tional Data Schedule F

. . . .

ITEM NOTES

ESTATE DATA

Proprietorship   Schedule

. . . .

1. Business or profession: _____ 2. Cash or accrual basis? _____

3. Is executor directed to continue business? _____ Authorized? _____ No instruction? _____

4. To whom does will leave business assets? _____

5. Earnings:

   19___ $ _____ ; 19___ $ _____ ; 19___ $ _____ ; 19___ $ _____ ;

   19___ $ _____ ; 19___ $ _____ ; 19___ $ _____ ; 19___ $ _____ ;
                                                  last three years: last five years:

   19___ $ _____ ; 19___ $ _____ ; $ _____ ; $ _____ .

6. Liquidated value of business? _____ Estimate? _____

ASSETS	INVENTORY VALUE	ESTIMATED SALVAGE
Cash	$ _____	$ _____
Accounts receivable	_____	_____
Inventory	_____	_____
Realty	_____	_____
Fixtures	_____	_____
Equipment	_____	_____
TOTALS	$ _____	$ _____

7. Liabilities:

Notes payable		$ _____
Accounts payable		_____
Wages		_____
Rentals		_____
Mortgages		_____
Other		_____
	TOTAL	$ _____

8. Any life insurance on key employees? _____

9. Is your life insured in favor of any employees? _____

10. Any employees capable of continuing the business after your withdrawal? _____
    If so, have you thought of: (a) incorporating and giving or selling them stock? _____
    (b) taking them into partnership? _____

11. Any employee benefit plans? _____ Pension? _____ *(Secure copy of pla*
    Profit-sharing? _____ How administered? _____ *(Secure copy of pl*

(overleaf for more space)

nal Data   Schedule G

·   · · · ·

M   NOTES

ESTATE DATA

Real Estate Schedu

. . . .

ITEM	STATE	VALUE	COST	INCOME	TAXES & MAINTENANCE	DEPRECIATION Annual	Cumulative	TITLE*

* If in joint name or that of another:

ITEM	TITLE	SOURCE OF PURCHASE PRICE	GIFT TAX FILED	TAX PAI

Mortgages Schedu

. . . .

ITEM	AMOUNT	INSURED	RATIO VALUE TO COST	INTEREST	AMORTIZATION	TYPE OF PROPERTY

ESTATE DATA

fe Insurance *

. . . .

LIFE OF	AMOUNT	BENEFICIARY	OWNER	SOURCE OF PREMIUMS	REVERSION TO INSURED?	TRANSFER?

All life insurance owned by, or on the life of, the client.

HOW TO USE THE ESTATE ORGANIZER FOR PROPERTY PLANNING

I.   ORGANIZATION: The Organizer is set up in five parts. The cover, which may be used as a file folder, is the basic Organizer and contains all that you will need for most cases: Family questionnaire (Schedule A), Assets (Schedule B), Liabilities (Schedule C).

If the particular client has substantial interests in particular kinds of property that necessarily give rise to special problems, use the proper added schedule. You will find these inside the basic Organizer: Personal and Estate Objectives (Schedule D), provided for those who do not use the Analagraph; Corporation (Schedule E), Partnership (Schedule F), Proprietorship (Schedule G), Real Estate (Schedule H), Mortgages (Schedule I), Life Insurance (Schedule J). The last three are all on one leaf.

II.   SCHEDULE A: Designed to give the family picture to enable coordinated planning and permit sensible flow of property.

        WILLS: Check for bequests inconsistent with trust provisions, business p/s agreements, insurance settlements, inter vivos gifts, joint ownership provisions, estate values themselves, ability to partition or liquidate property; ability of trustee to retain property; effects of community property interest of spouse, or upon business interests; also tax payment clauses, after-born children and identification of assets to be used as marital property.

        LIVING TRUSTS: Check for term, retention of rights or benefits, reversions (IRC '54, §§ 673 - 677); retained life interests, possibilities of reverter (IRC '54, § 2036); transfers taking effect at death (IRC '54, § 2037); possible use of income to discharge obligations of grantor (IRC '54, § 677); status as to Marital Deduction; powers of appointment.

        INSURANCE TRUSTS: Indicate when grantor and insured are not same person.

III.   SCHEDULE B: Designed to reveal three basic facts: present value, post-mortem value, current income value of assets. In item R, list Social Security benefits, Employee Benefit Plan participations, etc.

Community property should be properly allocated between the spouses in accordance with local law. Generally speaking, the community comprises property acquired or values created during marriage except that a gift, bequest, devise or inheritance becomes the separate property of the recipient.

The market value of a going business may be arrived at by a variety of methods. One, suggested by ARM 34, CB, June 1920, p. 31, capitalizes the excess of five years' average annual earnings over the aggregate of a reasonable return on net worth and a reasonable allowance for the services actually rendered by the owners; then adds that capitalized value back to net asset value. Such a value is apt to prevail for estate tax purposes if the business is to be continued beyond the death of the owner.

(i)

SCHEDULE C: Self-explanatory. Contingent liabilities must probably take client's estimate.

SCHEDULE D: Designed to reveal both needs and objectives. The former are set forth as minimums, the latter as desired benefits. Special or temporary income needs may often be provided by the same funds used for ultimate distribution to legatees of capital or to charities. Then consider use of trusts, insurance under interest option, and like devices.

For efficient integration of assets to produce income consider:

LIFE INSURANCE − − Option settlements.

BUSINESS INTERESTS*− − P/S Contract funded by life insurance payable under option settlements through the use of the trustee disclaimer provision. Retained limited partnership interests, common or preferred stock, may indicate a trust.

REAL ESTATE AND SECURITIES − − Trust, either testamentary or revocable living.

MISCELLANEOUS CASH AND QUICK ASSETS − − Trust, either living or testamentary, participating in a voluntary Common Trust Fund. Acceptable units usually from about $3,000 to $50,000 cash. Available in most states.

SCHEDULE E: Designed to reveal all facts needed to enable sound planning for liquidity, estate tax valuation pegs, key man needs, employee plan needs. In Item 6, indicate par value (if any) and specified yield as well as number of shares. Indicate preferences in liquidation or redemption. When stock is owned by any estate or trust, obtain: identity of decedent or grantor, identities of beneficiaries and the nature and extent of their interests, provisions of any trust instrument. If stock, held by "others", is owned by corporations or partnerships, identify their shareholders or members and obtain percentages of interest.

SCHEDULE F: See V., above. In Item 14, indicate general, special, or limited partners and whether the percentage of interest applies across the board or varies as to capital account and profit and loss.

SCHEDULE G: See V., above. Items 8, 9, 10 and 11 are designed to reveal a possible market for the proprietor's interest. Item 10 suggests means of giving employees incentives to stay with employer and purchasing power to fund P/S Contract.

SCHEDULE H: Designed to show all necessary facts regarding realty, including its drain upon − or contribution to − spending power of beneficiaries.

SCHEDULE I (at foot of schedule H): Self-explanatory.

SCHEDULE J (Reverse of schedule H): Self-explanatory. Secure policies. Beneficiary provisions must be checked for consistency with plan of disposition, qualification for marital deduction, after-born children, consistency with retirement uses of insurance, etc.

VALUATION SCHEDULES

BUSINESS LIQUIDATION VALUES

If the business is to be liquidated, its market value is its liquidation value. Depending upon the nature of the business, the ratio of liquidation value of assets to their book value may reasonably be figured thus:

Cash	100
Accounts Receivable	85-25
Inventory	100-35
Realty	100-50
Fixtures	50-10
Equipment	75-25

Non-traded close corporation stock derives its value from the underlying business. Thus it may reflect going concern value or merely the liquidation value of the aggregate assets. Hence the range shown in the table "Ratio: Conversion to Market Value" below.

CONVERSION VALUE

Post-mortem value is shown as Conversion Value — — the cash an executor may reasonably expect to get for the asset. Figure it thus:

ITEM	DESCRIPTION		RATIO: CONVERSION TO MARKET VALUE	NOTES
A			100	† owner's estimate
B			100	
C			100	* Cash payable plus discounted
D			90	value of principal instalments
E			90	deferred beyond valuation date.
F	common	) if high-grade investment	85	
		) if high-grade speculative	70	
	preferred		90	
G	high-grade		85	
	other		60	‡ liquidated value
H	high-grade		80	
	other		30	
I	high-grade		100	
	low-grade		70	
J			†	** Use care. General powers of
K	subject to)			appointment may be taken into
	P/S Contract)		*	estate at full conversion value,
	other		100-30	yet failure to exercise them
L	subject to)			may result in no assets or in-
	P/S Contract)		*	come for deceased's own ben-
	other		‡	eficiaries.
M	subject to)			
	P/S Contract)		*	
	other		‡	
N	based on under-)			
	lying assets)		100-30 **	
O			†	
P			100	
Q			100	
R			†	

Conversion ratios are somewhat arbitrary and assume experienced executors, who will realize more than amateurs.

ANALYSIS AND WORK SHEETS

FOR

PROPERTY PLANNING

Case No._____

Name:_____

Date:_____

INVENTORY, MARSHALLING AND CONVERSION OF ESTATE ASSETS

ASSETS INVENTORY	OWNER'S VALUE	VALUE & INCLUDIBILITY FOR TAX	CONVERSION VALUE	RETENTION VALUE	INCOME
Executor or Administrator					
1.					
2.					
3.					
4.					
5.					
6.					
7.					
8.					
9.					
10.					
11.					
12.					
13.					
14. Total					
15. Less Property Exempt From Administration					
16. Probate Estate					
Passing By Survivorship:					
17.					
18.					
19.					
20. Total Passing By Survivorship					
Passing By Trust, Contract, or Devise:					
21.					
22.					
23.					
24. Total Passing By Trust, Contract, or Devise					
25. Total General Property					
26. Life Insurance					
27. Interests In Estates					

ITEMS	AMOUNT	TOTALS	ITEMS	AMOUNT	TOTALS
Assets			**Liabilities**		
1. Cash on Hand and in Bank			Current Bills Payable		
2. Insurance Payable to Estate			Notes Payable		
3. Death Benefits or Annuities			Insurance Bank Loans		
4. Certificates of Deposit			Accrued Taxes:		
5. Cash Value of Policies on Other's Lives			(a) real and personal property		
			(b) income tax (state and federal)		
6. Notes Receivable (Collectible Value)			Funeral and Last Expense		
7. Accounts Receivable (Collectible Value)			Mortgages		
8. Converted Property			Miscellaneous		
9. Business Interest			Total Liabilities	xxxxxxx	
10. Total Cash	xxxxxxx				
Assets Sold					
11.			Widow's Allowance (If in Cash)	xxxxxxx	
12.			Administration Costs	xxxxxxx	
13.			Total State Tax		xxxxxxx
14.			U.S. Estate Tax		xxxxxxx
15.			Total Succession Taxes	xxxxxxx	
16.					
17.					
18.					
19.			Total Cash Bequests	xxxxxxx	
20. Total for Liquidation	xxxxxxx		Total Cash Requirements *	xxxxxxx	

* Total Cash Requirements .... $ _____

Total Cash Available (items 10 & 20) .... _____

Cash Surplus (or Deficit) .... _____

STATE INHERITANCE TAXES

Page 4.

NET TAXABLE ESTATE				ITEM	TAXABLE SHARES			
ITEM	PASSING BY WILL	PASSING BY TRUST	PASSING BY SURVIVORSHIP		TO SPOUSE	TO	TO	TO
Assets:				From Probate Estate:				
				Outright				
				Life Interests				
				Term Interests				
				Remainders				
				Other				
				Total				
				Passing By Trust:				
				Life Interests				
				Term Interests				
				Remainders				
				Total				
				Survivorship Shares:				
Totals								
Total Gross Estate:	xxxxxxx			Total Taxable Share				
Deductions:				Exemption				
				Net Taxable Share				
				Tax				

	STATE OF DOMICILE	OTHER STATES
TAXES		
Total Inheritance		
U.S. Estate Tax Credit (Apportioned)		xxxxxxxxxxxxxxxxx
Excess of Credit		xxxxxxxxxxxxxxxxx
State Estate		xxxxxxxxxxxxxxxxx
Total		xxxxxxxxxxxxxxxxx
Other States		

Total Deductions　　　xxxxxxx

DETERMINATION OF NET ESTATE AND COMPUTATION OF U. S. ESTATE TAX

ITEMS	A. SEPARATE PROPERTY	B. COMMUNITY PROPERTY
Gross Estate		
1. General Property		
2. Life Insurance		
3. Property Subject to Taxable Power		
4. Property in Trust		
5. Interests in Estates		
6. Total Gross Estate		
Deductions		
7. Funeral and Last Expenses		
8. Debts and Claims		
9. Mortgages and Liens		
10. Miscellaneous Deductions		
11. Administration Costs (Estimated at ____%)		
12. Sub-total		
13. Separate Property (Item 6A)	xxxxxxxxxxxxxx	xxxxxxxxxxxxxx
14. Total Community Property (Item 6B)	xxxxxxxxxxxxxx	
15. Less Proportionate Share of Item 12		
16. Adjusted Gross Estate		
17. Marital Deduction		
18. Spouse's Moiety (½ Community Property)	xxxxxxxxxxxxxx	xxxxxxxxxxxxxx
19. Charitable Bequests		
20. Specific Exemption		
21. Sub-total: Items 17, 19, and 20		
22. Net Taxable Estate (Item 16 less Item 21)		

COMPUTATION OF U. S. ESTATE TAX

23. Total Net Taxable Estate (22A + 22B)		
24. Gross Tentative U.S. Estate Tax		
25. Total Credits*		
26. Net U.S. Estate Taxes		
27. State Inheritance and Estate Taxes		
28. Total Succession Taxes		
29. Net Estate (Items 17, 20 and 23 minus Item 28)		

Credits:

State Taxes	
Gift Tax	
Prior Tax	
Foreign Tax	
Sub Total to Line 25	

POST-PROBATE ESTATE

ASSET	AMOUNT	FOR CONVERSION	FOR RETENTION	INCOME
1. Cash (surplus after liquidation)				
2. Government Bonds (total)				
3. Municipal Bonds (total)				
4. Securities: (listed and unlisted)				
(a) high grade bonds				
(b) low grade bonds				
(c) preferred stocks (high grade)				
(d) preferred stocks (low grade)				
(e) investment common stocks				
(f) speculative common stocks				
5. Mortgages				
6. Long-Term Notes				
7. Stock in Close Corporations				
(a)_____shares @ _____				
(b)_____shares @ _____				
(c)_____shares @ _____				
8. Partnership				
9. Proprietorship				
10 Realty:				
(a) home				
(b) residential rental				
(c) industrial rental				
(d) farms				
(e) non-productive				
11. Total Residual Estate				

ITEM	SPOUSE		CHILDREN	
	PRINCIPAL	INCOME	PRINCIPAL	INCOME
From Estate				
1. Cash				
2. Government Bonds				
3. Municipal Bonds				
4. Bonds (other than above)				
5. Stocks				
6. Mortgages and Long-Term Notes				
7. Living Trusts				
8. Realty				
9. Miscellaneous				
10. Sub Total				
11. Retained Business Interest				
12. Total From Estate				
Other Income of Beneficiaries				
13. Insurance:				
(a) reinvested lump-sum proceeds				
(b) proceeds under policy options				
14. Insurance Trusts:				
(a) cash				
(b)				
15. Stock in Decedent's Corporation				
16. Annuities				
17. Donated Property				
18. Securities				
19. Realty				
20. Father's Estate				
21. Mother's Estate				
22. Miscellaneous				
23. Total From Own Sources				
24. Total From All Sources				
25. Fixed Charges	XXXXXX		XXXXXX	
26. Net Income	XXXXXX		XXXXXX	
27. Aggregate Income Tax	XXXXXX		XXXXXX	
28. Adjustments *	XXXXXX		XXXXXX	
29. Spendable Income	XXXXXX		XXXXXX	
30. Income Requirement	XXXXXX		XXXXXX	

SUMMARY OF ANALYSIS AND SUGGESTED REVISIONS

TRANSFER OF PROPERTY AT DEATH	ORIGINAL ESTATE PLAN	REVISION NO.	REVISION NO.	REVISION NO.	REVISION NO.	REVISION NO.
1. Original Probate Estate						
2. Property Out of Probate						
3. Total Transferred						
4. Administration						
5. State Taxes						
6. U. S. Estate Taxes						
Summary of Transfer Costs						
7. Administration						
8. State Tax						
9. U. S. Estate Tax						
10. Total						
11. Gift Tax						
12. Net Saving	xxxxxxxx					
13. Cash Requirements						
14. Total Cash Available						
15. Surplus (or Deficit)						
Income Exhibit						
16. From Estate						
17. Income of Beneficiary						
18. Total Income						
19. Fixed Charges						
20. Net						
21. Income Tax						
22. Spendable Income						

INCOME EXHIBIT

PRESENT PLAN: Present income $ _____ ; less ( ) exemptions equals net income $ _____ ; minus tax $ _____ equals spendable income $ _____ .

REVISED PLAN	REVISION NO.	REVISION NO.	REVISION NO.	REVISION NO.
Income of Donor				
1. Present Income				
2. Less Income Transferred				
3. Revised Income				
4. Less ( ) Exemptions				
5. Revised Net Income				
6. Tax				
7. Spendable Income (#3 less #6)				
Income of Donee				
8. Present Income				
9. Add Income from Gift				
10. Total Income After Gift				
11. Exemption				
12. Net Income				
13. Tax				
14. Income after Tax				
15. Present Income of Donor (spendable income under present plan, above)				
16. Add: Item #7 $ _____ " #14 _____ TOTAL $ _____				
17. Saving (#16 less #15)				

Page 10.

REALTY SITUATED IN OTHER STATES

ITEM	STATE	TITLE	NET VALUE	COST	SOURCE OF PURCHASE PRICE	EXEMPTION OR DEDUCTION	TAX
1.							
2.							
3.							
4.							
5.							
6.							
7.							
8.							
9.							
10.							

TRUSTS OR CORPORATE SECURITIES SUBJECT TO MULTIPLE TAXATION

COMPANY	STATE OF INCORPORATION	RECIPROCITY BY STATUTE	TAXABLE VALUE	TAX
1.				
2.				
3.				
4.				
5.				
6.				
7.				
8.				
9.				
10.				

Page 11.

Of Special Significance:

ANNUAL REVIEW FOR 19___.

I. THE FAMILY:

A. EDUCATION:

	SON	DAUGHTER	GRANDCHILD	OTHER
Entering college	_____	_____	_____	_____
Completing college	_____	_____	_____	_____
Entering graduate school	_____	_____	_____	_____
Completing graduate school	_____	_____	_____	_____

B. PERSONALS:

A member of the family has:

	YES	NO
become engaged	_____	_____
been married	_____	_____
been born	_____	_____
been adopted	_____	_____
become disabled	_____	_____
been divorced	_____	_____
passed away	_____	_____
embarked on a career	_____	_____
retired	_____	_____

C. THE HOME:

Purchased _____   Sold _____

Mortgage redeemed _____   Mortgaged _____

II. THE BUSINESS:

	YES	NO
Any change in kind of business?	_____	_____
Have you formed (dissolved) a partnership?	_____	_____
Have you incorporated (liquidated a corporation)?	_____	_____
Added (dropped) a partner (co-stockholder)?	_____	_____
Lost a partner (co-stockholder) by disability (death)?	_____	_____
Employed any key people?	_____	_____
Established any Employee Benefit Plans?	_____	_____
Entered upon a planned program of expansion?	_____	_____

III. FINANCIAL ASPECTS:

	SELF	SPOUSE	SON	DAUGHTER
Earned income increased	_____	_____	_____	_____
Earned income decreased	_____	_____	_____	_____
Other income increased	_____	_____	_____	_____
Other income decreased	_____	_____	_____	_____

FINANCIAL ASPECTS (Continued). . . .

	SELF	SPOUSE	SON	DAUGHTE
Purchased/Sold:				
securities	_____	_____	_____	_____
government bonds	_____	_____	_____	_____
real estate	_____	_____	_____	_____
Started new bank accounts:				
savings	_____	_____	_____	_____
checking	_____	_____	_____	_____
custodial	_____	_____	_____	_____
Inherited property	_____	_____	_____	_____
Executed a new will	_____	_____	_____	_____
Established a trust	_____	_____	_____	_____
Made gifts, in trust or otherwise	_____	_____	_____	_____
Received gifts, in trust or otherwise	_____	_____	_____	_____
Matured/Paid-Up insurance	_____	_____	_____	_____
Surrendered/Lapsed insurance	_____	_____	_____	_____
Acquired/Lost Social Security coverage	_____	_____	_____	_____
Acquired/Lost Employee Plan benefits	_____	_____	_____	_____
Made a gain/loss in security values	_____	_____	_____	_____

IV. ADVISORS AND CUSTODIANS:

	NO CHANGE	NEW
My attorney is:	_____	_____
My accountant is:	_____	_____
My banker is:	_____	_____
My safe deposit box is at:	_____	_____

ESTATE ORGANIZER FOR PROPERTY PLANNING
(Condensed Form)
A. FINANCES

I. ASSETS	CLIENT	SPOUSE	II. LIABILITIES	CLIENT	SPOUSE
a. QUICK			Loans:		
Certificates of Deposit .... $	$		Insurance .... $	$	
Life Insurance:			Brokers'		
Self			Other		
Others			Mortgages		
Annuities:			Taxes:		
Self			Real Estate		
Others			Income		
Stocks			Personal Property		
Bonds			Other		
Business Interest, (if Funded P/S Contract)			Contingent Liabilities		
			Leasehold Liability:		
			Home		
			Business		
Sub-Total $	$		Total $	$	
b. SLOW					
Business Interest ... $	$				
Interests in Estates or Trusts					
Other					
Sub-Total $	$				

Excess (Deficiency), Quick Assets
over Liabilities (I.a. - II.) .... $
Plus or Minus Cash Bequests: ....
Net Excess (Deficiency) .... $

B. THE FAMILY

Item	The Client	Spouse, Children and Others			Remarks
Birth Date					
Legal Residence					
Health					
Separate Property					
Source?					
Salary					
Other Income					
Potential Inheritances:					
Source?					
Is there a will?*					
When and where made?					
In whose favor?					
Testamentary trust?					
Living Trusts*					
In favor of					
Value?					
Revocable?					
Gifts since 6/6/32:					
To whom?					
When?					
Value and nature?					
Return filed?					
Life Insurance:					
Own life					
Lives of others					

* Secure copy.

Page Two..........

C. THE CLIENT'S OBJECTIVES

I. Retirement at age: _____ ; financial only _____ ; physical _____

    Minimum monthly income for: (a) self and wife $ _____ ; (b) survivor: (1) self $ _____

    (2) wife $ _____

II Estate (all incomes monthly):

	TO WIFE		TO OTHERS	
'Till youngest child self-supporting ... $		_____ for ____ years: $		
Life income thereafter		_____ for ____ years:		
Adjustment for _____ years		_____ for ____ years:		
Other		_____ for ____ years:		
Sub-Total	$		$	

SPECIAL FUNDS

Invasion $ _____ ; annual withdrawal $ _____ ; ( ) cumulative,   ( ) non-cumulative.

Education $ _____ for _____ for _____

              _____ for _____ for _____

              _____ for _____ for _____

              _____ for _____ for _____

Mortgage Cancellation .... $

Other:

NAME	PURPOSE	AMOUNT
_____	_____	_____
_____	_____	_____
_____	_____	_____
_____	_____	_____

THE AUTHOR

George Byron Gordon is Director of Advanced Underwriting Services for The Mutual Benefit Life Insurance Company; consulting editor of Prentice-Hall, Inc.; member of the Editorial Board of the ESTATE PLANNERS QUARTERLY; a director of the Newark, New Jersey, Chapter of Profit-Sharing Industries; and former executive editor of Prentice-Hall, Inc. He is the author and co-author of several books, listed elsewhere in this book, and of numerous articles.

Trained in the law and in economics, he was educated at universities here and abroad and is a specialist on estate planning, business organization and federal tax matters.

He has taught insurance and legal subjects, been guest lecturer at the University of Connecticut, the University of Georgia, the University of Kansas, Seton Hall University, Louisiana State University, the University of Florida, the University of Illinois, the Financial Public Relations Association, the N.Y.U. Institute on Federal Taxation, the Tulane Tax Institute, the Rutgers Tax Institute, the Practising Law Institute (N.Y.), the American Management Association and is a frequent speaker before bar and trust groups, C.L.U. chapters, Life Underwriters Associations, Estate Planning Councils and Life Insurance and Trust Councils through the country.

INDEX